EDUCATION IN A COMPETITIVE AND GLOBALIZING WORLD SERIES

SUCCESS IN MATHEMATICS EDUCATION

Rural Education in the 21st Century
Christine M.E. Frisiras (Editor)
2009. ISBN: 978-1-60692-966-7

IT- Based Project Change Management System
Faisal Manzoor Arain and Low Sui Pheng
2009. ISBN: 978-1-60741-148-2

Reading: Assessment, Comprehension and Teaching
Nancy H. Salas and Donna D. Peyton (Editors)
2009. ISBN: 978-1-60692-615-4

Reading: Assessment, Comprehension and Teaching
Nancy H. Salas and Donna D. Peyton (Editors)
2009. ISBN: 978-1-60876-543-0 (Online Book)

Mentoring: Program Development, Relationships and Outcomes
Michael I. Keel (Editor)
2009. ISBN: 978-1-60692-287-3

Mentoring: Program Development, Relationships and Outcomes
Michael I. Keel
2009. ISBN: 978-1-60876-727-4 (Online Book)

Enhancing Prospects of Longer-Term Sustainability of Cross-Cultural INSET Initiatives in China
Chunmei Yan
2009. ISBN: 978-1-60741-615-9

Multimedia in Education and Special Education
Onan Demir and Cari Celik
2009. ISBN: 978-1-60741-073-7

PCK and Teaching Innovations
Syh-Jong Jang
2009. ISBN: 978-1-60741-147-5

Academic Administration: A Quest for Better Management and Leadership in Higher Education
Sheying Chen (Editor)
2009. ISBN: 978-1-60741-732-3

New Research in Education: Adult, Medical and Vocational
Edmondo Balistrieri and Giustino DeNino (Editors)
2009. ISBN: 978-1-60741-873-3

**Approaches to Early Childhood
and Elementary Education**
Francis Wardle
2009. ISBN: 978-1-60741-643-2

Recent Trends in Education
Borislav Kuzmanović and Adelina Cuevas (Editors)
2009. ISBN: 978-1-60741-795-8

Expanding Teaching and Learning Horizons in Economic Education
Franklin G. Mixon, Jr. and Richard J. Cebula
2009. ISBN: 978-1-60741-971-6

**Challenges of Quality Education
in Sub-Saharan African Countries**
Daniel Namusonge Sifuna and Nobuhide Sawamura
2010. ISBN: 978-1-60741-509-1

Developments in Higher Education
Mary Lee Albertson (Editor)
2010. ISBN: 978-1-60876-113-5

**The Process of Change in Education: Moving from Descriptive to Prescriptive
Research**
Baruch Offir
2010. ISBN: 978-1-60741-451-3

Success in Mathematics Education
Caroline B. Baumann (Editor)
2009. ISBN: 978-1-60692-299-6

EDUCATION IN A COMPETITIVE AND GLOBALIZING WORLD SERIES

SUCCESS IN MATHEMATICS EDUCATION

CAROLINE B. BAUMANN
EDITOR

Nova Science Publishers, Inc.
New York

For permission to use material from this book please contact us:
Telephone 631-231-7269; Fax 631-231-8175
Web Site: http://www.novapublishers.com

NOTICE TO THE READER

The Publisher has taken reasonable care in the preparation of this book, but makes no expressed or implied warranty of any kind and assumes no responsibility for any errors or omissions. No liability is assumed for incidental or consequential damages in connection with or arising out of information contained in this book. The Publisher shall not be liable for any special, consequential, or exemplary damages resulting, in whole or in part, from the readers' use of, or reliance upon, this material. Any parts of this book based on government reports are so indicated and copyright is claimed for those parts to the extent applicable to compilations of such works.

Independent verification should be sought for any data, advice or recommendations contained in this book. In addition, no responsibility is assumed by the publisher for any injury and/or damage to persons or property arising from any methods, products, instructions, ideas or otherwise contained in this publication.

This publication is designed to provide accurate and authoritative information with regard to the subject matter covered herein. It is sold with the clear understanding that the Publisher is not engaged in rendering legal or any other professional services. If legal or any other expert assistance is required, the services of a competent person should be sought. FROM A DECLARATION OF PARTICIPANTS JOINTLY ADOPTED BY A COMMITTEE OF THE AMERICAN BAR ASSOCIATION AND A COMMITTEE OF PUBLISHERS.

LIBRARY OF CONGRESS CATALOGING-IN-PUBLICATION DATA

Success in mathematics education / [edited by] Caroline B. Baumann.
    p. cm.
Includes bibliographical references and index.
ISBN 978-1-60692-299-6 (hardcover)
1. Mathematics--Study and teaching--United States. I. Baumann, Caroline B.
QA13.S8845 2009
372.7--dc22
                                                                    2009028862

Published by Nova Science Publishers, Inc. ✛ *New York*

CONTENTS

Contents

PREFACE

The eminence, safety, and well-being of nations have been entwined for centuries with the ability of their people to deal with sophisticated quantitative ideas. Leading societies have commanded mathematical skills that have brought them advantages in medicine and health, in technology and commerce, in navigation and exploration, in defense and finance, and in the ability to understand past failures and to forecast future developments. This book explores the actions that must be taken to strengthen the American people in this central area of learning. Success matters to the nation at large and to its individual students and families, because it opens doors and creates opportunity. Much of this book on mathematics and science in the United States focuses on national economic competitiveness and the economic well-being of citizens and enterprises.

Chapter 1 - The eminence, safety, and well-being of nations have been entwined for centuries with the ability of their people to deal with sophisticated quantitative ideas. Leading societies have commanded mathematical skills that have brought them advantages in medicine and health, in technology and commerce, in navigation and exploration, in defense and finance, and in the ability to understand past failures and to forecast future developments. History is full of examples.

During most of the 20th century, the United States possessed peerless mathematical prowess—not just as measured by the depth and number of the mathematical specialists who practiced here but also by the scale and quality of its engineering, science, and financial leadership, and even by the extent of mathematical education in its broad population. But without substantial and sustained changes to its educational system, the United States will relinquish its leadership in the 21st century. This report is about actions that must be taken to strengthen the American people in this central area of learning. Success matters to the nation at large. It matters, too, to individual students and their families, because it opens doors and creates opportunities.

Chapter 2 - Because mathematics education bears on the policy concerns delineated in the preceding section, the President created the National Mathematics Advisory Panel in April 2006 via Executive Order 13398 (Appendix A). He assigned responsibility to the U.S. Secretary of Education for appointment of members and for oversight.

The Panel's precise charge, given in the Executive Order, is to advise the President and the Secretary on ways "...to foster greater knowledge of and improved performance in mathematics among American students...with respect to the conduct, evaluation, and effective use of the results of research relating to proven-effective and evidence-based mathematics instruction." The Executive Order further calls for recommendations "...based on the best available scientific evidence." Moreover, the Executive Order also defines a particular set of topics for the Panel to examine:

Chapter 3 - This Panel, diverse in experience, expertise, and philosophy, agrees broadly that the delivery system in mathematics education—the system that translates mathematical knowledge into value and ability for the next generation—is broken and must be fixed. This is not a conclusion about teachers or school administrators, or textbooks or universities or any other single element of the system. It is about how the many parts do not now work together to achieve a result worthy of this country's values and ambitions.

On the basis of its deliberation and research, the Panel can report that America has genuine opportunities for improvement in mathematics education. This report lays them out for action.

Chapter 4 - To clarify instructional needs in Grades K–8 and to sharpen future discussion about the role of school algebra in the overall mathematics curriculum, the Panel made a specific effort to delineate the content and demands of *school algebra*, which is the term used here to encompass the full body of algebraic material that the Panel expects to be covered through high school, regardless of its organization into courses and levels. Most commonly, school algebra is organized into two courses, Algebra I and II. Less commonly, the content of school algebra is interwoven with that of geometry, trigonometry, statistics, and other mathematical subjects in an *integrated curriculum* covering several courses in high school. Even when the traditional pattern of Algebra I and II is used, the course called Algebra II may include elements of statistics or trigonometry in place of some of the more advanced elements of school algebra, which may be offered in a subsequent precalculus course. When the Panel addressed the effective preparation of students for the study of Algebra, its expectation was that students should be able to proceed successfully at least through the content of Algebra II, wherever the elements might be taught in the high school curriculum.

Chapter 5 – The mathematics that children learn from preschool through the middle grades provides the basic foundation for Algebra and more advanced mathematics course work. Even before they enter kindergarten, most children develop considerable knowledge of numbers and other aspects of mathematics. The mathematical knowledge that children bring to school influences their math learning for many years thereafter, and probably throughout their education.

When they enter kindergarten, most children from families with the combination of low-parental education levels, low incomes, and single parents bring less foundational knowledge for learning school mathematics than does the average child from more advantaged backgrounds. Fortunately, a variety of promising instructional programs have been developed to improve the mathematical knowledge of preschoolers and kindergartners, especially those from at-risk backgrounds, and have yielded encouraging results.

Chapter 6 – Substantial differences in mathematics achievement of students are attributable to differences in teachers. Teachers are crucial to students' opportunities to learn and to their learning of mathematics.

There are large, measurable differences in the effectiveness of mathematics teachers in generating achievement gains:

Chapter 7 - A controversial issue in the field of mathematics education is whether classroom instruction should be more teacher directed or more student centered. These terms encompass a wide array of meanings, with teacher-directed instruction ranging from highly scripted direct instruction approaches to interactive lecture styles, and with student-centered instruction ranging from students having primary responsibility for their own mathematics learning to highly structured cooperative groups. Schools and districts must make choices about curricular materials and instructional approaches that often seem more aligned with one instructional orientation than another. This leaves teachers wondering about when to organize their instruction one way or the other, whether certain topics are taught more effectively with one approach or another, and whether certain students benefit more from one approach than another.

Chapter 8 - One would like to assume that textbooks for middle school and high school mathematics are free of errors. But when mathematicians have reviewed recently published middle and high school textbooks, they have identified many errors and a large number of ambiguous and confusing statements and problems. One such review of widely used Algebra I textbooks was conducted on behalf of the Panel. Many of the detected errors and ambiguities arose in word problems that were intended to elicit use of the mathematical concepts and procedures in "real-world" contexts.

Chapter 9 - Achievement tests are widely used to estimate what students know and can do in specific subject areas. Tests make visible to teachers, parents, and policymakers some of the outcomes of student learning. They also can drive instruction. Due to their important role in education today, the Panel examined released items from the mathematics portions of the NAEP and six state tests and reviewed the relevant scientific literature on the appropriate content of such tests, the setting of performance categories (e.g., by determining cut scores), and factors affecting the quality of measurement, accuracy, and appropriate test design.

Chapter 10 - Systematic reviews of research on mathematics education by the task groups and subcommittees of the Panel yielded thousands of studies on important topics, but only a small proportion met standards for rigor for the causal questions the Panel was attempting to answer. The dearth of relevant rigorous research in the field is a concern. First, the number of experimental studies in education that can provide answers to questions of cause and effect is currently small. Although the number of such studies has grown in recent years due to changes in policies and priorities at federal agencies, these studies are only beginning to yield findings that can inform educational policy and practice. Second, in educational research over the past two decades, the pendulum has swung sharply away from quantitative analyses that permit inferences from samples to populations. Third, there is a need for a stronger emphasis on such aspects of scientific rigor as operational definitions of constructs, basic research to clarify phenomena and constructs, and disconfirmation of hypotheses. Therefore, debates about issues of national importance, which mainly concern cause and effect, have devolved into matters of personal opinion rather than scientific evidence.

LIST OF ABBREVIATIONS

ABCTE	American Board for Certification of Teacher Excellence
ACT	American College Testing
CAI	Computer-Assisted Instruction ETS Educational Testing Service
IDA STPI	Institute for Defense Analyses Science and Technology Policy Institute
LA	Low Achieving
LD	Learning Disabilities
NAEP	National Assessment of Educational Progress
NCTM	National Council of Teachers of Mathematics
NES	National Evaluation Systems
NVS	NAEP Validity Study
SES	Socioeconomic Status
STEM	Science, Technology, Engineering, and Mathematics
TAI	Team Assisted Individualization
TIMSS	Trends in International Mathematics and Science Study
PISA	Programme for International Student Assessment

ACKNOWLEDGMENTS

The members of the National Mathematics Advisory Panel express the greatest appreciation to those who facilitated this work, beginning with our own employers. This work of the Panel required extraordinary time commitments over a two-year period, and the gifts of that time represent substantial, concrete support for this project by the institutions that employ the members. They are recognized with gratitude below.

This report was developed and adopted by the panelists listed on page vii, who constituted the membership at the end of the project. During the two years of the Panel's work, there were changes in membership caused by shifts in personal and professional circumstances and by the Panel's direct request for augmentation in particular areas of expertise. Appendix B is a list of all members ever appointed to the Panel. Here, the concluding members wish to express appreciation for the contributions of colleagues who were once part of the Panel: Nancy Ichinaga, Diane Auer Jones, Thomas W. Luce, III, and Kathie Olsen.

From time to time, the Panel was fortunate to be able to call on the specific expertise of many colleagues. They examined materials as needed, offered opinions on specialized topics, and examined drafts of sections. We thank them all for their able and generous contributions: Mark Ashcraft, Richard A. Askey, Scott K. Baker, Arthur J. Baroody, Hyman Bass, Benjamin Samuel Clarke, Carol S. Dweck, Anne Foegen, Karen C. Fuson, Dan Goldhaber, Thomas L. Good, Eric A. Hanushek, James Hiebert, Heather C. Hill, Roger Howe, Andrew G. Izsak, Nancy C. Jordan, Jeremy Kilpatrick, Kenneth R. Koedinger, W. James Lewis, David F. Lohman, R. James Milgram, Anthony Ralston, William H. Schmidt, Catherine Sophian, Jon R. Star, Joyce VanTassel-Baska, Patrick W. Thompson, Johannes E.H. Van Luit, Linda Dager Wilson, and Bradley Witzel. Of course, the Panel itself is responsible for the language, findings, and recommendations in this report.

The budget dedicated to this project by the U.S. Department of Education was augmented by funds from donors who are also recognized below. Their generosity enabled work that was more thorough and more expertly supported than would ever have been otherwise possible.

Finally, the Panel expresses the deepest appreciation to the U.S. Department of Education staff, headed by Executive Director Tyrrell Flawn. They carried out essential tasks with skill and dedication. Without them, this report would have not been realized.

EXECUTIVE SUMMARY

Background

The eminence, safety, and well-being of nations have been entwined for centuries with the ability of their people to deal with sophisticated quantitative ideas. Leading societies have commanded mathematical skills that have brought them advantages in medicine and health, in technology and commerce, in navigation and exploration, in defense and finance, and in the ability to understand past failures and to forecast future developments. History is full of examples.

During most of the 20th century, the United States possessed peerless mathematical prowess—not just as measured by the depth and number of the mathematical specialists who practiced here but also by the scale and quality of its engineering, science, and financial leadership, and even by the extent of mathematical education in its broad population. But without substantial and sustained changes to its educational system, the United States will relinquish its leadership in the 21st century. This report is about actions that must be taken to strengthen the American people in this central area of learning. Success matters to the nation at large. It matters, too, to individual students and their families, because it opens doors and creates opportunities.

Much of the commentary on mathematics and science in the United States focuses on national economic competitiveness and the economic well-being of citizens and enterprises. There is reason enough for concern about these matters, but it is yet more fundamental to recognize that the safety of the nation and the quality of life—not just the prosperity of the nation—are at issue.

> *During most of the 20   h century, the United States possessed peerless mathematical prowess—not just as measured by the depth and number of the mathematical specialists who practiced here, but also by the scale and quality of its engineering, science, and financial leadership....*

In the contemporary world, an educated technical workforce undergirds national leadership. Yet the United States faces a future in which there will be accelerating retirements affecting a large fraction of the current science and engineering workforce, even as the growth of job opportunities in this sector is expected to outpace job growth in the economy at large. These trends will place substantial stress on the nation's ability to sustain a workforce with adequate scale and quality. For many years, our country has imported a great volume of technical talent from abroad, but the dramatic success of economies overseas in the age of the Internet casts doubt on the viability of such a strategy in the future, because attractive employment for technical workers is developing in countries that have been supplying invaluable talent for U.S. employers. From 1990 to 2003, research and development expenditures in Asian countries other than Japan grew from an insignificant percentage to almost half of American R&D expenditures. There are consequences to a weakening of American independence and leadership in mathematics, the natural sciences, and engineering. We risk our ability to adapt to change. We risk technological surprise to our economic viability and to the foundations of our country's security. National policy must ensure the healthy development of a domestic technical workforce of adequate scale with top-level skills.

But the concerns of national policy relating to mathematics education go far beyond those in our society who will become scientists or engineers. The national workforce of future years will surely have to handle quantitative concepts more fully and more deftly than at present. So will the citizens and policy leaders who deal with the public interest in positions of civic leadership. Sound education in mathematics across the population is a national interest.

Success in mathematics education also is important for individual citizens, because it gives them college and career options, and it increases prospects for future income. A strong grounding in high school mathematics through Algebra II or higher correlates powerfully with access to college, graduation from college, and earning in the top quartile of income from employment. The value of such preparation promises to be even greater in the future. The National Science Board indicates that the growth of jobs in the mathematics-intensive science and engineering workforce is outpacing overall job growth by 3:1.

> *International and domestic comparisons show that American students have not been succeeding in the mathematical part of their education at anything like a level expected of an international leader.*

International and domestic comparisons show that American students have not been succeeding in the mathematical part of their education at anything like a level expected of an international leader. Particularly disturbing is the consistency of findings that American students achieve in mathematics at a mediocre level by comparison to peers worldwide. On our own "National Report Card"—the National Assessment of Educational Progress (NAEP)—there are positive trends of scores at Grades 4 and 8, which have just reached historic highs. This is a sign of significant progress. Yet other results from NAEP are less positive: 32% of our students are at or above the "proficient" level in Grade 8, but only 23% are proficient at Grade 12. Consistent with these findings is the vast and growing demand for remedial mathematics education among arriving students in four-year colleges and community colleges across the nation.

Moreover, there are large, persistent disparities in mathematics achievement related to race and income—disparities that are not only devastating for individuals and families but also project poorly for the nation's future, given the youthfulness and high growth rates of the largest minority populations.

Although our students encounter difficulties with many aspects of mathematics, many observers of educational policy see Algebra as a central concern.[1] The sharp falloff in mathematics achievement in the U.S. begins as students reach late middle school, where, for more and more students, algebra course work begins. Questions naturally arise about how students can be best prepared for entry into Algebra.

These are questions with consequences, for Algebra is a demonstrable gateway to later achievement. Students need it for any form of higher mathematics later in high school; moreover, research shows that completion of Algebra II correlates significantly with success in college and earnings from employment. In fact, students who complete Algebra II are more than twice as likely to graduate from college compared to students with less mathematical preparation. Among African-American and Hispanic students with mathematics preparation at least through Algebra II, the differences in college graduation rates versus the student population in general are half as large as the differences for students who do not complete Algebra II.

For all of these considerations, the President created the National Mathematics Advisory Panel in April 2006, with the responsibilities of relying upon the "best available scientific evidence" and recommending ways "...to foster greater knowledge of and improved performance in mathematics among American students."

> ***Students who complete Algebra II are more than*** *twice as likely to graduate from college compared to students with less mathematical preparation.*

PRINCIPAL MESSAGES

This Panel, diverse in experience, expertise, and philosophy, agrees broadly that the delivery system in mathematics education—the system that translates mathematical knowledge into value and ability for the next generation—is broken and must be fixed. This is not a conclusion about any single element of the system. It is about how the many parts do not now work together to achieve a result worthy of this country's values and ambitions.

On the basis of its deliberation and research, the Panel can report that America has genuine opportunities for improvement in mathematics education. This report lays them out for action.

The essence of the Panel's message is *to put first things first*. There are six elements, expressed compactly here, but in greater detail later.

- The mathematics curriculum in Grades PreK–8 should be streamlined and should emphasize a well-defined set of the most critical topics in the early grades.
- Use should be made of what is clearly known from rigorous research about how children learn, especially by recognizing a) the advantages for children in having a strong start; b) the mutually reinforcing benefits of conceptual understanding, procedural fluency, and automatic (i.e., quick and effortless) recall of facts; and c) that effort, not just inherent talent, counts in mathematical achievement.
- Our citizens and their educational leadership should recognize mathematically knowledgeable classroom teachers as having a central role in mathematics education and should encourage rigorously evaluated initiatives for attracting and appropriately preparing prospective teachers, and for evaluating and retaining effective teachers.
- Instructional practice should be informed by high-quality research, when available, and by the best professional judgment and experience of accomplished classroom teachers. High-quality research does not support

the contention that instruction should be either entirely "student centered" or "teacher directed." Research indicates that some forms of particular instructional practices can have a positive impact under specified conditions.

- NAEP and state assessments should be improved in quality and should carry increased emphasis on the most critical knowledge and skills leading to Algebra.
- The nation must continue to build capacity for more rigorous research in education so that it can inform policy and practice more effectively.

Positive results can be achieved in a reasonable time at accessible cost, but a consistent, wise, community-wide effort will be required. Education in the United States has many participants in many locales—teachers, students, and parents; state school officers, school board members, superintendents, and principals; curriculum developers, textbook writers, and textbook editors; those who develop assessment tools; those who prepare teachers and help them to continue their development; those who carry out relevant research; association leaders and government officials at the federal, state, and local levels. All carry responsibilities. All can be important to success.

The network of these many participants is linked through interacting national associations. A coordinated national approach toward improved mathematics education will require an annual forum of their leaders for at least a decade. The Panel recommends that the U.S. Secretary of Education take the lead in convening the forum initially, charge it to organize in a way that will sustain an effective effort, and request a brief annual report on the mutual agenda adopted for the year ahead.

The President asked the Panel to use the best available scientific research to advise on improvements in the mathematics education of the nation's children. Our consistent respect for sound research has been the main factor enabling the Panel's joint conclusions on so many matters, despite differences of perspective and philosophy. At the same time, we found no research or insufficient research relating to a great many matters of concern in educational policy and practice. In those areas, the Panel has been very limited in what it can report.

The Panel lays out many concrete steps that can be taken now toward significantly improved mathematics education, but it also views them only as a best start in a long process. This journey, like that of the post-Sputnik era, will require a commitment to "learning as we go along." The nation should recognize that there is much more to discover about how to achieve better results. Models of continuous improvement have proven themselves in many other areas, and they can work again for America in mathematics education.

THE NATIONAL MATHEMATICS ADVISORY PANEL

The President established the Panel via Executive Order 13398 (Appendix A), in which he also assigned responsibility to the U.S. Secretary of Education for appointment of members and for oversight of the Panel. While the presidential charge contains many explicit elements, there is a clear emphasis on the preparation of students for entry into, and success in, Algebra.

Over a period of 20 months, the Panel received public testimony as a committee of the whole but worked largely in task groups and subcommittees dedicated to major components of the presidential charge. Questions like the following illustrate the scope of the Panel's inquiry:

- What is the essential content of school algebra and what do children need to know before starting to study it?
- What is known from research about how children learn mathematics?
- What is known about the effectiveness of instructional practices and materials?
- How can we best recruit, prepare, and retain effective teachers of mathematics?
- How can we make assessments of mathematical knowledge more accurate and more useful?
- What do practicing teachers of algebra say about the preparation of students whom they receive into their classrooms and about other relevant matters?
- What are the appropriate standards of evidence for the Panel to use in drawing conclusions from the research base?.

Each of five task groups carried out a detailed analysis of the available evidence in a major area of the Panel's responsibility: Conceptual Knowledge and Skills, Learning Processes, Instructional Practices, Teachers and Teacher

Education, and Assessment. Each of three subcommittees was charged with completion of a particular advisory function for the Panel: Standards of Evidence, Instructional Materials, and the Panel-commissioned National Survey of Algebra Teachers (see sidebar, page 9). Each task group and subcommittee produced a report supporting this document. All eight reports are separately available.

The Panel took consistent note of the President's emphasis on "the best available scientific evidence" and set a high bar for admitting research results into consideration. In essence, the Panel required the work to have been carried out in a way that manifested rigor and could support generalization at the level of significance to policy. One of the subcommittee reports covers global considerations relating to standards of evidence, while individual task group reports amplify the standards in the particular context of each task group's work. In all, the Panel reviewed more than 16,000 research publications and policy reports and received public testimony from 110 individuals, of whom 69 appeared before the Panel on their own and 41 others were invited on the basis of expertise to cover particular topics. In addition, the Panel reviewed written commentary from 160 organizations and individuals, and analyzed survey results from 743 active teachers of algebra.

In late 2007, the Panel synthesized this Final Report by drawing together the most important findings and recommendations, which are hereby issued with the Panel's full voice. This report connects in many places to the eight reports of the task groups and subcommittees, which carry detailed analyses of research literature and other relevant materials. These supporting reports cover work carried out as part of the Panel's overall mission, but they are presented by only those members who participated in creating them. This Final Report represents findings and recommendations of the Panel as a whole.

> ***The Panel took consistent note of the President's*** *emphasis on "the best available scientific evidence" and set a high bar for admitting research results into consideration.*

Main Findings and Recommendations

The Panel had a broad scope and reached many individual findings and recommendations, all conveyed in the main report under headings corresponding to those below. This Executive Summary generally contains only abbreviated versions of the most important points.

Curricular Content

1. A focused, coherent progression of mathematics learning, with an emphasis on proficiency with key topics, should become the norm in elementary and middle school mathematics curricula. Any approach that continually revisits topics year after year without closure is to be avoided. By the term *focused*, the Panel means that curriculum must include (and engage with adequate depth) the most important topics underlying success in school algebra. By the term *coherent*, the Panel means that the curriculum is marked by effective, logical progressions from earlier, less sophisticated topics into later, more sophisticated ones. Improvements like those suggested in this report promise immediate positive results with minimal additional cost.

   By the term *proficiency*, the Panel means that students should understand key concepts, achieve automaticity as appropriate (e.g., with addition and related subtraction facts), develop flexible, accurate, and automatic execution of the standard algorithms, and use these competencies to solve problems.[2]

2. To clarify instructional needs in Grades PreK–8 and to sharpen future discussion about the role of school algebra in the overall mathematics curriculum, the Panel developed a clear concept of school algebra via its list of Major Topics of School Algebra (Table 1, page 16).

School algebra is a term chosen to encompass the full body of algebraic material that the Panel expects to be covered through high school, regardless of its organization into courses and levels. The Panel expects students to be able to proceed successfully at least through the content of Algebra II.

3. The Major Topics of School Algebra in Table 1 should be the focus for school algebra standards in curriculum frameworks, algebra courses, textbooks for algebra, and in end-of-course assessments.

4. A major goal for K–8 mathematics education should be proficiency with fractions (including decimals, percent, and negative fractions), for such proficiency is foundational for algebra and, at the present time, seems to be severely underdeveloped. Proficiency with whole numbers is a necessary precursor for the study of fractions, as are aspects of measurement and geometry. These three areas—whole numbers, fractions, and particular aspects of geometry and measurement—are the Critical Foundations of Algebra. Important elements within each of these three categories are delineated on page 17 of this report.

    The Critical Foundations are not meant to comprise a complete mathematics curriculum leading to algebra; however, they deserve primary attention and ample time in any mathematics curriculum.

5. To encourage the development of students in Grades PreK–8 at an effective pace, the Panel recommends a set of Benchmarks for the Critical Foundations (Table 2, page 20). They should be used to guide classroom curricula, mathematics instruction, textbook development, and state assessments.

6. All school districts should ensure that all prepared students have access to an authentic algebra course—and should prepare more students than at present to enroll in such a course by Grade 8. The word *authentic* is used here as a descriptor of a course that addresses algebra consistently with the Major Topics of School Algebra (Table 1, page 16). Students must be prepared with the mathematical prerequisites for this course according to the Critical Foundations of Algebra (page 17) and the Benchmarks for the Critical Foundations (Table 2, page 20).

7. Teacher education programs and licensure tests for early childhood teachers, including all special education teachers at this level, should fully address the topics on whole numbers, fractions, and the appropriate geometry and measurement topics in the Critical Foundations of Algebra, as well as the concepts and skills leading to them; for elementary teachers, including elementary level special education teachers, all topics

in the Critical Foundations of Algebra and those topics typically covered in an introductory Algebra course; and for middle school teachers, including middle school special education teachers, the Critical Foundations of Algebra and all of the Major Topics of School Algebra.

Learning Processes

8. Most children acquire considerable knowledge of numbers and other aspects of mathematics before they enter kindergarten. This is important, because the mathematical knowledge that kindergartners bring to school is related to their mathematics learning for years thereafter—in elementary school, middle school, and even high school. Unfortunately, most children from low-income backgrounds enter school with far less knowledge than peers from middle-income backgrounds, and the achievement gap in mathematical knowledge progressively widens throughout their PreK–12 years.

9. Fortunately, encouraging results have been obtained for a variety of instructional programs developed to improve the mathematical knowledge of preschoolers and kindergartners, especially those from low-income backgrounds. There are effective techniques—derived from scientific research on learning—that could be put to work in the classroom today to improve children's mathematical knowledge. However, tests of both short-term and long-term effects of these interventions with larger populations of children from low-income families are urgently needed.

10. To prepare students for Algebra, the curriculum must simultaneously develop conceptual understanding, computational fluency, and problem-solving skills. Debates regarding the relative importance of these aspects of mathematical knowledge are misguided. These capabilities are mutually supportive, each facilitating learning of the others. Teachers should emphasize these interrelations; taken together, conceptual understanding of mathematical operations, fluent execution of procedures, and fast access to number combinations jointly support effective and efficient problem solving.

11. Computational proficiency with whole number operations is dependent on sufficient and appropriate practice to develop automatic recall of addition and related subtraction facts, and of multiplication and related division facts. It also requires fluency with the standard algorithms for

addition, subtraction, multiplication, and division. Additionally it requires a solid understanding of core concepts, such as the commutative, distributive, and associative properties. Although the learning of concepts and algorithms reinforce one another, each is also dependent on different types of experiences, including practice.

12. Difficulty with fractions (including decimals and percent) is pervasive and is a major obstacle to further progress in mathematics, including algebra. A nationally representative sample of teachers of Algebra I who were surveyed for the Panel rated students as having very poor preparation in "rational numbers and operations involving fractions and decimals."

As with learning whole numbers, a conceptual understanding of fractions and decimals and the operational procedures for using them are mutually reinforcing. One key mechanism linking conceptual and procedural knowledge is the ability to represent fractions on a number line. The curriculum should afford sufficient time on task to ensure acquisition of conceptual and procedural knowledge of fractions and of proportional reasoning. Instruction focusing on conceptual knowledge of fractions is likely to have the broadest and largest impact on problem-solving performance when it is directed toward the accurate solution of specific problems.

13. Mathematics performance and learning of groups that have traditionally been underrepresented in mathematics fields can be improved by interventions that address social, affective, and motivational factors. Recent research documents that social and intellectual support from peers and teachers is associated with higher mathematics performance for all students, and that such support is especially important for many African-American and Hispanic students. There is an urgent need to conduct experimental evaluations of the effectiveness of support-focused interventions both small- and large-scale, because they are promising means for reducing the mathematics achievement gaps that are prevalent in U.S. society.

14. Children's goals and beliefs about learning are related to their mathematics performance. Experimental studies have demonstrated that changing children's beliefs from a focus on ability to a focus on effort increases their engagement in mathematics learning, which in turn improves mathematics outcomes: When children believe that their efforts to learn make them "smarter," they show greater persistence in mathematics learning. Related research demonstrates that the engagement

and sense of efficacy of African-American and Hispanic students in mathematical learning contexts not only tends to be lower than that of white and Asian students but also that it can be significantly increased. Teachers and other educational leaders should consistently help students and parents to understand that an increased emphasis on the importance of effort is related to improved mathematics performance. This is a critical point because much of the public's self-evident resignation about mathematics education (together with the common tendencies to dismiss weak achievement and to give up early) seems rooted in the erroneous idea that success is largely a matter of inherent talent or ability, not effort.

15. Teachers and developers of instructional materials sometimes assume that students need to be a certain age to learn certain mathematical ideas. However, a major research finding is that what is developmentally appropriate is largely contingent on prior opportunities to learn. Claims based on theories that children of particular ages cannot learn certain content because they are "too young," "not in the appropriate stage," or "not ready" have consistently been shown to be wrong. Nor are claims justified that children cannot learn particular ideas because their brains are insufficiently developed, even if they possess the prerequisite knowledge for learning the ideas.

Teachers and Teacher Education

16. Teachers who consistently produce significant gains in students' mathematics achievement can be identified using value-added analyses (analyses that examine individual students' achievement gains as a function of the teacher). The impact on students' mathematics learning is compounded if students have a series of these more effective teachers Unfortunately, little is known from existing high-quality research about what effective teachers do to generate greater gains in student learning. Further research is needed to identify and more carefully define the skills and practices underlying these differences in teachers' effectiveness, and how to develop them in teacher preparation programs.

17. Research on the relationship between teachers' mathematical knowledge and students' achievement confirms the importance of teachers' content knowledge. It is self-evident that teachers cannot teach what they do not know. However, because most studies have relied on proxies for teachers' mathematical knowledge (such as teacher certification or

courses taken), existing research does not reveal the specific mathematical knowledge and instructional skill needed for effective teaching, especially at the elementary and middle school level. Direct assessments of teachers' actual mathematical knowledge provide the strongest indication of a relation between teachers' content knowledge and their students' achievement. More precise measures are needed to specify in greater detail the relationship among elementary and middle school teachers' mathematical knowledge, their instructional skill, and students' learning.

18. Teaching well requires substantial knowledge and skill. However, existing research on aspects of teacher education, including standard teacher preparation programs, alternative pathways into teaching, support programs for new teachers (e.g., mentoring), and professional development, is not of sufficient rigor or quality to permit the Panel to draw conclusions about the features of professional training that have effects on teachers' knowledge, their instructional practice, or their students' achievement.

    Currently there are multiple pathways into teaching. Research indicates that differences in teachers' knowledge and effectiveness between these pathways are small or nonsignificant compared to very large differences among the performance of teachers within each pathway.

19. The mathematics preparation of elementary and middle school teachers must be strengthened as one means for improving teachers' effectiveness in the classroom. This includes preservice teacher education, early career support, and professional development programs. A critical component of this recommendation is that teachers be given ample opportunities to learn mathematics for teaching. That is, teachers must know in detail and from a more advanced perspective the mathematical content they are responsible for teaching and the connections of that content to other important mathematics, both prior to and beyond the level they are assigned to teach.

    High-quality research must be undertaken to create a sound basis for the mathematics preparation of elementary and middle school teachers within preservice teacher education, early-career support, and ongoing professional development programs. Outcomes of different approaches should be evaluated by using reliable and valid measures of their effects on prospective and current teachers' instructional techniques and, most importantly, their effects on student achievement.

20. In an attempt to improve mathematics learning at the elementary level, a number of school districts around the country are using "math specialist teachers" of three different types—math coaches (lead teachers), full-time elementary mathematics teachers, and pull-out teachers. However, the Panel found no high-quality research showing that the use of any of these types of math specialist teachers improves students' learning.

    The Panel recommends that research be conducted on the use of full-time mathematics teachers in elementary schools. These would be teachers with strong knowledge of mathematics who would teach mathematics full-time to several classrooms of students, rather than teaching many subjects to one class, as is typical in most elementary classrooms. This recommendation for research is based on the Panel's findings about the importance of teachers' mathematical knowledge. The use of teachers who have specialized in elementary mathematics teaching could be a practical alternative to increasing all elementary teachers' content knowledge (a problem of huge scale) by focusing the need for expertise on fewer teachers.

21. Schools and teacher education programs should develop or draw on a variety of carefully evaluated methods to attract and prepare teacher candidates who are mathematically knowledgeable and to equip them with the skills to help students learn mathematics.

22. Research on teacher incentives generally supports their effectiveness, although the quality of the studies is mixed. Given the substantial number of unknowns, policy initiatives involving teacher incentives should be carefully evaluated.

Instructional Practices

23. All-encompassing recommendations that instruction should be entirely "student centered" or "teacher directed" are not supported by research. If such recommendations exist, they should be rescinded. If they are being considered, they should be avoided. High-quality research does not support the exclusive use of either approach.

24. Research has been conducted on a variety of cooperative learning approaches. One such approach, Team Assisted Individualization (TAI), has been shown to improve students' computation skills. This highly structured pedagogical strategy involves heterogeneous groups of students helping each other, individualized problems based on

student performance on a diagnostic test, specific teacher guidance, and rewards based on both group and individual performance. Effects of TAI on conceptual understanding and problem solving were not significant.

25. Teachers' regular use of formative assessment improves their students' learning, especially if teachers have additional guidance on using the assessment to design and to individualize instruction. Although research to date has only involved one type of formative assessment (that based on items sampled from the major curriculum objectives for the year, based on state standards), the results are sufficiently promising that the Panel recommends regular use of formative assessment for students in the elementary grades.

26. The use of "real-world" contexts to introduce mathematical ideas has been advocated, with the term "real world" being used in varied ways. A synthesis of findings from a small number of high-quality studies indicates that if mathematical ideas are taught using "real-world" contexts, then students' performance on assessments involving similar "real-world" problems is improved. However, performance on assessments more focused on other aspects of mathematics learning, such as computation, simple word problems, and equation solving, is not improved.

27. Explicit instruction with students who have mathematical difficulties has shown consistently positive effects on performance with word problems and computation. Results are consistent for students with learning disabilities, as well as other students who perform in the lowest third of a typical class. By the term *explicit instruction*, the Panel means that teachers provide clear models for solving a problem type using an array of examples, that students receive extensive practice in use of newly learned strategies and skills, that students are provided with opportunities to think aloud (i.e., talk through the decisions they make and the steps they take), and that students are provided with extensive feedback.

This finding does not mean that all of a student's mathematics instruction should be delivered in an explicit fashion. However, the Panel recommends that struggling students receive some explicit mathematics instruction regularly. Some of this time should be dedicated to ensuring that these students possess the foundational skills and conceptual knowledge necessary for understanding the mathematics they are learning at their grade level.

28. Research on instructional software has generally shown positive effects on students' achievement in mathematics as compared with instruction that does not incorporate such technologies. These studies show that technology-based drill and practice and tutorials can improve student performance in specific areas of mathematics. Other studies show that teaching computer programming to students can support the development of particular mathematical concepts, applications, and problem solving.

    However, the nature and strength of the results vary widely across these studies. In particular, one recent large, multisite national study found no significant effects of instructional tutorial (or tutorial and practice) software when implemented under typical conditions of use. Taken together, the available research is insufficient for identifying the factors that influence the effectiveness of instructional software under conventional circumstances.

29. A review of 11 studies that met the Panel's rigorous criteria (only one study less than 20 years old) found limited or no impact of calculators on calculation skills, problem solving, or conceptual development over periods of up to one year. This finding is limited to the effect of calculators as used in the 11 studies. However, the Panel's survey of the nation's algebra teachers indicated that the use of calculators in prior grades was one of their concerns. The Panel cautions that to the degree that calculators impede the development of automaticity, fluency in computation will be adversely affected.

    The Panel recommends that high-quality research on particular uses of calculators be pursued, including both their short- and long-term effects on computation, problem solving, and conceptual understanding.

30. Mathematically gifted students with sufficient motivation appear to be able to learn mathematics much faster than students proceeding through the curriculum at a normal pace, with no harm to their learning, and should be allowed to do so.

Instructional Materials

31. U.S. mathematics textbooks are extremely long—often 700–1,000 pages. Excessive length makes books more expensive and can contribute to a lack of coherence. Mathematics textbooks are much smaller in many nations with higher mathematics achievement than the U.S., thus

demonstrating that the great length of our textbooks is not necessary for high achievement. Representatives of several publishing companies who testified before the Panel indicated that one substantial contributor to the length of the books was the demand of meeting varying state standards for what should be taught in each grade. Other major causes of the extreme length of U.S. mathematics textbooks include the many photographs, motivational stories, and other nonmathematical content that the books include. Publishers should make every effort to produce much shorter and more focused mathematics textbooks.

32. States and districts should strive for greater agreement regarding which topics will be emphasized and covered at particular grades. Textbook publishers should publish editions that include a clear emphasis on the material that these states and districts agree to teach in specific grades.

33. Publishers must ensure the mathematical accuracy of their materials. Those involved with developing mathematics textbooks and related instructional materials need to engage mathematicians, as well as mathematics educators, at all stages of writing, editing, and reviewing these materials.

Assessment

34. NAEP and state tests for students through Grade 8 should focus on and adequately represent the Panel's Critical Foundations of Algebra. Student achievement on this critical mathematics content should be reported and tracked over time.

35. The Panel suggests that the NAEP strand on "Number Properties and Operations" be expanded and divided into two parts. The former should include a focus on whole numbers, including whole number operations (i.e., addition, subtraction, multiplication, division), at Grade 4, and on all integers (negative and positive) at Grade 8. The second content area involving number should focus on fractions. At Grade 4, it should involve beginning work with fractions and decimals, including recognition, representation, and comparing and ordering. The coverage should be expanded to include operations with fractions, decimals, and percent at Grade 8. Similarly, the content of work with whole numbers and fractions on state tests should expand and cover these concepts and operations as they develop from year to year, particularly at Grades 5, 6, and 7, which are grade levels when the NAEP test is not offered.

36. The Panel recommends a more appropriate balance in how algebra is defined and assessed at both the Grade 4 and Grade 8 levels of the NAEP. The Panel strongly recommends that "algebra" problems involving patterns should be greatly reduced in these tests. The same consideration applies to state tests.

37. State tests and NAEP must be of the highest mathematical and technical quality. To this end, states and NAEP should develop procedures for item development, quality control, and oversight to ensure that test items reflect the best item-design features, are of the highest mathematical and psychometric quality, and measure what is intended, with non-construct-relevant sources of variance in performance minimized (i.e., with nonmathematical sources of influence on student performance minimized).

38. Calculators should not be used on test items designed to assess computational facility.

Research Policies and Mechanisms

39. It is essential to produce methodologically rigorous scientific research in crucial areas of national need, such as the teaching and learning of mathematics. Researchers, educators, state and federal policymakers, private foundations, and research agencies have made and can continue to make important contributions toward this goal. Specifically, more research is needed that identifies: 1) effective instructional practices, materials, and principles of instructional design, 2) mechanisms of learning, 3) ways to enhance teachers' effectiveness, including teacher education, that are directly tied to objective measures of student achievement, and 4) item and test features that improve the assessment of mathematical knowledge. Although the number of such studies has grown in recent years due to changes in policies and priorities at federal agencies, these studies are only beginning to yield findings, and their number remains comparatively small.

40. As in all fields of education, the large quantity of studies gathered in literature searches on important topics in mathematics education is reduced appreciably once contemporary criteria for rigor and generalizability are applied. Therefore, the Panel recommends that governmental agencies that fund research give priority not only to increasing the supply of research that addresses mathematics education

but also to ensuring that such projects meet stringent methodological criteria, with an emphasis on the support of studies that incorporate randomized controlled designs (i.e., designs where students, classrooms, or schools are randomly assigned to conditions and studied under carefully controlled circumstances) or methodologically rigorous quasi-experimental designs. These studies must possess adequate statistical power, which will require substantial funding.

Both smaller-scale experiments on the basic science of learning and larger-scale randomized experiments examining effective classroom practices are needed to ensure the coherent growth of research addressing important questions in mathematics education. Basic research on causal mechanisms of learning, as well as randomized trials, are essential, and, depending on their methodologies, both can be rigorous and relevant to educational practice. Basic research, in particular, is necessary to develop explicit predictions and to test hypotheses, which are underemphasized in current research on mathematics education.

41. Leaders of graduate programs in education and related fields should ensure attention to research design, analysis, and interpretation for teachers and those entering academic and educational leadership positions in order to increase the national capacity to conduct and utilize rigorous research.

42. New funding should be provided to establish support mechanisms for career shifts (K, or career development, awards from the National Institutes of Health represent one example). Many accomplished researchers who study the basic components of mathematics learning are not directly engaged in relevant educational research. While this more basic kind of research is important both in its own right and as a crucial foundation for designing classroom-level learning projects, at least some of these investigators have the potential to make more directly relevant contributions to educational research. Consequently, providing incentives for them to change the emphasis of their research programs could enhance research capacity in the field.

43. Support should be provided to encourage the creation of cross-disciplinary research teams, including expertise in educational psychology, sociology, economics, cognitive development, mathematics, and mathematics education.

44. PreK–12 schools should be provided with incentives and resources to provide venues for, and encourage collaboration in, educational research.

45. Unnecessary barriers to research should be lowered. Although existing guidelines for the protection of human subjects must be fully respected, Institutional Review Board procedures should be streamlined for educational research that qualifies as being of low or minimal risk. The resolutions of the National Board for Education Sciences concerning making individual student data available to researchers with appropriate safeguards for confidentiality should be supported.

End Notes

[1] The word "algebra" is capitalized when referring to a particular course or course sequence, such as Algebra I and II.

[2] This meaning is in keeping with *Adding It Up* (National Research Council, 2001, p. 116), in which five attributes were associated with the concept of proficiency: 1) conceptual understanding (comprehension of mathematical concepts, operations, and relations), 2) procedural fluency (skills in carrying out procedures flexibly, fluently, and appropriately), 3) strategic competence (ability to formulate, represent, and solve mathematical problems), 4) adaptive reasoning (capacity for logical thought, reflection, explanation, and justification), and 5) productive disposition (habitual inclination to see mathematics as sensible, useful, and worthwhile, coupled with a belief in diligence and one's own efficacy).

In: Success in Mathematics Education
Editor: Caroline B. Baumann

ISBN: 978-1-60692-299-6
© 2009 Nova Science Publishers, Inc.

Chapter 1

BACKGROUND FOR THE PRESIDENT'S CHARGE

United States Department of Education

The eminence, safety, and well-being of nations have been entwined for centuries with the ability of their people to deal with sophisticated quantitative ideas. Leading societies have commanded mathematical skills that have brought them advantages in medicine and health, in technology and commerce, in navigation and exploration, in defense and finance, and in the ability to understand past failures and to forecast future developments. History is full of examples.

During most of the 20th century, the United States possessed peerless mathematical prowess—not just as measured by the depth and number of the mathematical specialists who practiced here but also by the scale and quality of its engineering, science, and financial leadership, and even by the extent of mathematical education in its broad population. But without substantial and sustained changes to its educational system, the United States will relinquish its leadership in the 21st century. This report is about actions that must be taken to strengthen the American people in this central area of learning. Success matters to the nation at large. It matters, too, to individual students and their families, because it opens doors and creates opportunities.

Much of the commentary on mathematics and science in the United States focuses on national economic competitiveness and the economic well-being of citizens and enterprises. There is reason enough for concern about these matters, but it is yet more fundamental to recognize that the safety of the nation and the quality of life—not just the prosperity of the nation—are at issue.

> *During most of the 20th century, the United States possessed peerless mathematical prowess—not just as measured by the depth and number of the mathematical specialists who practiced here, but also by the scale and quality of its engineering, science, and financial leadership....*

In the contemporary world, an educated technical workforce undergirds national leadership. Yet the United States faces a future in which a large fraction of the current science and engineering workforce will be retiring. In the latest analysis, based on data from 2003, 26% of the science and engineering degree holders in the workforce (40% of doctoral degree holders) were age 50 or older (National Science Board, 2008). At the same time, the demand for employees in this sector is expected to outpace job growth in the economy at large. In the last decade for which Census data are available (1990 to 2000), growth in employment in science and engineering occupations tripled that in other occupations (National Science Board, 2008). The combination of retirements and increasing demand for technologically knowledgeable workers will stress the nation's ability to sustain a workforce of adequate scale and quality. We are not the first to note this danger (National Science Board, 2003).

For many years, the United States has imported a great volume of technical talent from abroad. Census data show that our domestic reliance on scientists and engineers from abroad significantly increased from 1990 to 2000—from 14% to 22% across the whole technical workforce and from 24% to 38% at the doctoral level. The dramatic success of economies overseas in the age of the Internet casts doubt on the viability of such a strategy in the future, because attractive employment for technical workers is developing in countries that have been supplying invaluable talent for U.S. employers. This point is underscored by the rapid growth of research and development (R&D) expenditures in China, Singapore, South Korea, and Taiwan. From 1990 to 2004, the volume of R&D in these four countries increased from an insignificant percentage to almost half of American R&D expenditures (National Science Foundation, 2007). By 2004, China's expenditures alone nearly reached parity with Japan's, and each country was funding R&D at about a third of the commitment in the U.S. (National Science Foundation, 2007).[1]

There are consequences to a weakening of U.S. independence and leadership in mathematics, the natural sciences, and engineering. Looking at the fast pace of technological advancement in the United States, Schacht (2005) commented, "[I]t is widely accepted that technological progress is responsible for up to one-half the growth of the U.S. economy, and is one principal driving force in long-term growth and increases in living standards." Ignoring threats to the nation's ability to advance in the science, technology, engineering, and mathematics (STEM) fields will put our economic viability and our basis for security at risk.

For decades, the education pipeline has not produced the necessary number of U.S. students for jobs in the STEM fields—jobs that the National Science Board indicates are outpacing overall job growth by 3:1 (National Science Board, 2008). As a result of this shortfall of citizens going into these fields, the United States has relied increasingly on immigrant and temporary nonimmigrant scientists and engineers (National Science Board, 2008). The fraction of U.S. students pursuing STEM-related degrees, according to recent numbers from the General Accountability Office (Ashby, 2006), has declined from 32% in academic year 1994–95 to 27% in academic year 2003–04. In addition, a report by the Commission on Professionals in Science and Technology stated, "[O]ver the past 40 years, there has been a significant decrease in the proportion of doctorates earned by U.S. citizens and permanent residents in STEM fields. In 1966, they earned 83.5% of all STEM doctorates awarded, but in 2004, they earned just 59.8%" (Babco, 2006). This strategy may not work in the future, however, because the supply of immigrant and temporary nonimmigrant STEM professionals may become more uncertain for reasons addressed above. It is therefore in the national interest to increase the number of domestic students studying and receiving degrees in STEM areas.

National policy must ensure the healthy development of a domestic technical workforce with adequate scale and top-level skill. But the concerns of national policy relating to mathematics education go well beyond those in our society who will become scientists or engineers. The national workforce of future years will surely have to handle quantitative concepts more fully and more deftly than at present. So will the citizens and policy leaders who deal with the public interest in positions of civic leadership. Sound education in mathematics across the population is a national interest.

Mathematics literacy is a serious problem in the United States. According to Philips (2007), 78% of adults cannot explain how to compute the interest paid on a loan, 71% cannot calculate miles per gallon on a trip, and 58% cannot calculate a 10% tip for a lunch bill. Further, it is clear from the research that a broad range of students and adults also have difficulties with fractions (e.g., Hecht, Vagi, & Torgeson, 2007; Mazzocco & Devlin, in press), a foundational skill essential to success in algebra. The recent National Assessment of Educational Progress

(NAEP, "the Nation's Report Card") shows that 27% of eighth-graders could not correctly shade 1/3 of a rectangle and 45% could not solve a word problem that required dividing fractions (U.S. Department of Education, 2004).

> *National policy must ensure the healthy development of a domestic technical workforce with adequate scale and top-level skill.*

Labor economists Richard J. Murnane and Frank Levy have spoken to the vital importance of mathematical skill (Murnane & Levy, 1996):

> *Close to half of all seventeen year olds cannot read or do math at the level needed to get a job at a modern automobile plant. Barring some other special knowledge or talent that would allow them to earn a living as, say, a plumber or artist, they lack the skills to earn a middle-class paycheck in today's economy.*

Algebra has emerged as a central concern, for it is a demonstrable gateway to later achievement. Students need Algebra[2] for more advanced mathematics course work in high school (Evan, Gray, & Olchefske, 2006). Yet, problems in mathematics learning in the U.S. increase in late middle school before students move into algebra. We see this in the scores on the NAEP. Results at Grade 4 have improved considerably over the past 15 years and have just reached historic highs; scores at Grade 8 have also increased somewhat; but no progress is evident at Grade 12. In addition, NAEP results show that only 39% of our students are at or above the "proficient" level in Grade 8 (U.S. Department of Education, 2007), and even fewer, 23%, are at that level by Grade 12 (U.S. Department of Education, 2005).

International comparisons also show that American students have not been succeeding in the mathematical part of their education at anything like a level expected of an international leader. In the Trends in Mathematics and Science Study (TIMSS), an international assessment, U.S. students do less well in Grade 8 than Grade 4. The performance is still poorer in Grade 12, although the data for Grade 12, dating from 1995, are now quite old (Evan et al., 2006). Similarly, in the 2007 Programme for International Student Assessment (PISA), U.S. 15-year-olds ranked 25th among 30 developed nations in math literacy and problem solving (Baldi, Jin, Shemer, Green, Hergert, & Xie, 2007). Even in elementary school, the U.S. is not among the world leaders; only 7% of U.S. fourth-graders scored at the advanced level in TIMSS, compared to 38% of fourth-graders in Singapore, a world leader in mathematics achievement.

From all of these results and analyses, questions naturally arise about how American students can be generally better prepared in mathematics and, in particular, how they can make a good start in secondary education by being well prepared for entry into Algebra.

Given the importance of mathematics education, we must also take a hard look at who will be teaching this subject in school. All the efforts to ensure that mathematics is given the attention it deserves in the nation's schools will be for naught without an adequate supply of mathematically knowledgeable and properly trained mathematics teachers.

Success in mathematics education matters at the level of individual citizens because it opens options for college and career and increases prospects for future income. The probability that a student will enroll in a four-year college correlates substantially with completion of high school mathematics programs beyond the level of Algebra II (Horn & Nuñez, 2000; Horowitz, 2005). In fact, students who complete Algebra II are more than twice as likely to graduate from college as students who lack such preparation (Adelman, 1999; Evan et al., 2006). Although such correlations do not establish cause-and-effect linkages, they are clear and notable, because they connect with policy concerns of leaders and practical choices that students and parents must make. College participation and graduation rates are critical for our nation, because college graduates offer many benefits to civic life and to the economy rooted in their additional education. College graduates are more likely to vote, use new technology, and become civic leaders, and are less likely to be involved in criminal activity (Pascarella & Terenzini, 1991).

Consistent with the NAEP findings is the vast and growing demand for remedial mathematics education among arriving students in four-year colleges and community colleges across the nation. Data from the year 2000 showed that 71% of America's degree-granting institutions offered an average of 2.5 remedial courses[3] in mathematics (Business Higher Education Forum, 2005). This need for remediation reveals weakness in the preparation of students for college and may limit a student's ability to advance toward a degree in a timely manner. Moreover, there are large, persistent disparities in mathematics achievement related to race and income—disparities that are not only devastating for individuals and families but also project poorly for the nation's future, given the youthfulness and high growth rates of the largest minority populations.

Attending college is a social escalator. It levels opportunities for success across all socioeconomic groups (Pascarella & Terenzini, 1991). Among students from the principal ethnic and racial groups in the U.S. who have completed mathematics courses at least through Algebra II, the differences in college graduation rates versus the student population in general are half as large as the differences for students who do not complete Algebra II (Achieve, Inc., 2006). According to research, "The achievement gap between students of differing ethnic and socioeconomic groups can be significantly reduced or even eliminated if low-income and minority students increase their success in high school mathematics and science courses" (Evan et al., 2006, p. 11).

Once out of college, an individual's past participation in mathematics courses and higher education continues to be correlated with benefits. Individuals who receive college degrees earn more and have better career mobility (McGregor, 1994). The majority of workers who earn more than $40,000 annually have two or more high school credits at the Algebra II level or higher (Achieve, Inc., 2006). A national poll found that more than two-thirds of students who took Algebra II in high school reported that they were well-prepared for demands of the workplace (Carnevale & Desrochers, 2003).

No longer can we accept that a rigorous mathematics education is reserved for the few who will go on to be engineers or scientists. Mathematics may indeed be "the new literacy" (Schoenfeld, 1995); at the least, it is essential for any citizen who is to be prepared for the future.

End Notes

[1] These data are Gross Expenditures on Research and Development, as defined by the OECD. This quantity comprises the total expenditure on R&D by all domestic enterprises, including businesses, institutes, universities, and government laboratories. R&D expenditures performed abroad by domestic enterprises are not included.

[2] The word "algebra" is capitalized when referring to a particular course or course sequence, such as Algebra I and II.

[3] Remedial courses cover precollegiate mathematics and normally do not bear credit that can be counted toward graduation from college. Some institutions do not offer remedial course work.

In: Success in Mathematics Education
Editor: Caroline B. Baumann

ISBN: 978-1-60692-299-6
© 2009 Nova Science Publishers, Inc.

Chapter 2

THE NATIONAL MATHEMATICS ADVISORY PANEL

United States Department of Education

Because mathematics education bears on the policy concerns delineated in the preceding section, the President created the National Mathematics Advisory Panel in April 2006 via Executive Order 13398 (Appendix A). He assigned responsibility to the U.S. Secretary of Education for appointment of members and for oversight.

The Panel's precise charge, given in the Executive Order, is to advise the President and the Secretary on ways "…to foster greater knowledge of and improved performance in mathematics among American students…with respect to the conduct, evaluation, and effective use of the results of research relating to proven-effective and evidence-based mathematics instruction." The Executive Order further calls for recommendations "…based on the best available scientific evidence." Moreover, the Executive Order also defines a particular set of topics for the Panel to examine:

a) the critical skills and skill progressions for students to acquire competence in algebra and readiness for higher levels of mathematics; b) the role and appropriate design of standards and assessment in promoting mathematical competence; c) the processes by which students of various abilities and backgrounds learn mathematics; d) instructional practices, programs, and materials that are effective for improving mathematics learning; e) the training, selection, placement, and professional development of teachers of mathematics in order to enhance students' learning of mathematics; f) the role and appropriate design of systems for delivering instruction in mathematics that combine the different elements of learning processes, curricula, instruction, teacher training and support, and standards, assessments, and accountability; g) needs for research in support of mathematics education; h) ideas for strengthening capabilities to teach children and youth basic mathematics, geometry, algebra, and calculus and other mathematical disciplines; i) such other matters relating to mathematics education as the Panel deems appropriate; and j) such other matters relating to mathematics education as the Secretary may require.

The first item in the President's list indicates that the Panel's focus should be on the preparation of students for entry into and success in algebra, which itself is a foundation for higher mathematics. Thus, the Panel has seen its role as addressing the teaching and learning of mathematics from preschool (PreK) through Grade 8 or so, with a particular emphasis on the concepts and skills most relevant to the learning of algebra.

Over a period of 20 months, the Panel received public testimony as a committee of the whole but worked largely in task groups and subcommittees. Each of five task groups carried out a detailed analysis of the available evidence in a major area of the Panel's responsibility: Conceptual Knowledge and Skills, Learning Processes, Instructional Practices, Teachers and Teacher Education, and Assessment. Each of three subcommittees was charged with completion of a particular advisory function for the Panel: Standards of Evidence, Instructional Materials, and the Panel-commissioned National Survey of Algebra Teachers (National Mathematics Advisory Panel, 2008; see sidebar, page 9).

> *The first item in the President's list indicates that the Panel's focus should be on the preparation of students for entry into and success in algebra, which itself is a foundation for higher mathematics.*

The task groups and subcommittees produced reports supporting this document. Those reports cover work carried out as part of the Panel's overall mission, but they are presented by only those members who participated in creating them. This Final Report represents findings and recommendations formally adopted by the Panel as a whole. All eight reports[1] are separately available in printed form and via the Web site that houses the Panel's work.[2]

Details of the Panel's work can be found in Appendixes B–E, which cover the membership and processes of the Panel.

VOICES FROM THE FIELD: WHAT ALGEBRA TEACHERS SAY

To understand the experiences of Algebra teachers in the classroom, the National Math Panel commissioned a national survey of randomly chosen Algebra I teachers designed to elicit their views on student preparation, work-related attitudes and challenges, and use of instructional materials. The National Opinion Research Center at the University of Chicago conducted the survey in the spring and summer of 2007. Of the 310 public schools identified, 258 agreed to participate, and 743 teachers—a 72% response rate—completed the questionnaire.

The survey revealed that teachers rate their students' background preparation for Algebra I as weak. The three areas in which teachers report their students to have the poorest preparation are rational numbers, word problems, and study habits. When asked to provide a brief description of any changes they would like to see in the curriculum leading up to Algebra I, teachers most often cited the need for a greater focus at the elementary school level on proficiency with basic mathematical concepts and skills.

Sample responses representing this predominant view include:

- "Students need to be better prepared in basic math skills and not be quite so calculator dependent. Also, more training in thinking skills."
- "Make sure the 1st–8th grade teachers teach the foundations of math and that the students know their basic skills."
- "More focus on basics—students should already know order of operations, positive vs. negative numbers, fractions and decimals."

With regard to instructional materials, teachers, for the most part, do not regularly use technological tools. On average, teachers said they use these tools less than once a week. Low levels of computer use do not appear to be a reflection of insufficient access. About one-third of teachers never use the graphing calculator, and manipulative materials are used only occasionally.

In response to 10 options describing the challenges they face, a majority of the teachers (62%) rated "working with unmotivated students" as the "single most challenging aspect of teaching Algebra I successfully." Their second highest-rated challenge—11%—was making mathematics accessible and comprehensible. However, the written-in responses most frequently mentioned handling different skill levels in a single classroom. A substantial number of teachers consider mixed-ability groupings to be a "moderate" (30%) or "serious" (23%) problem, an item with a combined rating of 53% for "moderate" and "serious," second only to the combined rating of 64% for "too little parent/family support."

The survey results reinforce the research findings presented in this report, particularly the need to strengthen students' proficiency with rational numbers. Further, the Panel suggests that greater attention be focused on ways in which negative attitudes toward mathematics develop and how to overcome students' lack of motivation.

A full report on the survey is available (National Mathematics Advisory Panel, 2008).

The Panel wishes to express its appreciation to the teachers who participated in this survey. Their voices and experience proved valuable to the Panel's work.

The Panel took consistent note of the President's emphasis on "the best available scientific evidence" and set a high bar for admitting research results into consideration. In essence, the Panel required the work to have been carried out in a way that manifested rigor and could support generalization at the level of significance to policy. One of the subcommittee reports covers global considerations relating to standards of evidence, while individual task group reports amplify the standards in the particular context of each task group's work.

In all, the Panel reviewed more than 16,000 research publications and policy reports and received public testimony from 110 individuals, of whom 69 appeared before the Panel on their own and 41 others were invited on the basis of expertise to cover particular topics. Those who testified included parents, teachers, school administrators, members of boards of education, educational researchers, textbook publishers, and other individuals interested in improving mathematics education. In addition, the Panel reviewed written commentary from 160 organizations and individuals, and analyzed survey results from 743 active teachers of algebra.

In late 2007, the Panel synthesized this Final Report by drawing together the most important findings and recommendations. They are hereby issued with the Panel's full voice. This report connects in many places to the eight reports of the task groups and subcommittees, which carry detailed analyses of research literature and other relevant materials. The sections below are not extensively referenced, because the goal of this report is to communicate the Panel's main conclusions without distractions from detail. Readers interested in a particular topic should examine the relevant task group and subcommittee reports.

End Notes

[1] National Mathematics Advisory Panel (2008).
[2] http://www.ed.gov/mathpanel.

In: Success in Mathematics Education
Editor: Caroline B. Baumann

ISBN: 978-1-60692-299-6
© 2009 Nova Science Publishers, Inc.

Chapter 3

PRINCIPAL MESSAGES

United States Department of Education

This Panel, diverse in experience, expertise, and philosophy, agrees broadly that the delivery system in mathematics education—the system that translates mathematical knowledge into value and ability for the next generation—is broken and must be fixed. This is not a conclusion about teachers or school administrators, or textbooks or universities or any other single element of the system. It is about how the many parts do not now work together to achieve a result worthy of this country's values and ambitions.

On the basis of its deliberation and research, the Panel can report that America has genuine opportunities for improvement in mathematics education. This report lays them out for action.

FIRST THINGS FIRST

The essence of the Panel's message is *to put first things first*. There are six elements, expressed compactly here, but in greater detail later.

- The mathematics curriculum in Grades PreK–8 should be streamlined and should emphasize a well-defined set of the most critical topics in the early grades.
- Use should be made of what is clearly known from rigorous research about how children learn, especially by recognizing a) the advantages for

children in having a strong start; b) the mutually reinforcing benefits of conceptual understanding, procedural fluency, and automatic (i.e., quick and effortless) recall of facts; and c) that effort, not just inherent talent, counts in mathematical achievement.

- Our citizens and their educational leadership should recognize mathematically knowledgeable classroom teachers as having a central role in mathematics education and should encourage rigorously evaluated initiatives for attracting and appropriately preparing prospective teachers, and for evaluating and retaining effective teachers.
- Instructional practice should be informed by high-quality research, when available, and by the best professional judgment and experience of accomplished classroom teachers. High-quality research does not support the contention that instruction should be either entirely "student-centered" or "teacher-directed." Research indicates that some forms of particular instructional practices can have a positive impact under specified conditions.
- NAEP and state assessments should be improved in quality and should carry increased emphasis on the most critical knowledge and skills leading to Algebra.
- The nation must continue to build capacity for more rigorous research in education so that it can inform policy and practice more effectively.

Positive results can be achieved in a reasonable time at accessible cost, but a consistent, wise, community-wide effort will be required. Education in the United States has many participants in many locales—teachers, students, and parents; state school officers, school board members, superintendents, and principals; curriculum developers, textbook writers, and textbook editors; those who develop assessment tools; those who prepare teachers and help them to continue their development; those who carry out relevant research; association leaders and government officials at the federal, state, and local levels. All carry responsibilities. All are important to success.

The network of these participants is linked through interacting national associations. A coordinated national approach toward improved mathematics education will require an annual forum of their leaders for at least a decade. The Panel recommends that the U.S. Secretary of Education take the lead in convening the forum initially, charge it to organize in a way that will sustain an effective effort, and request a brief annual report on the mutual agenda adopted for the year ahead.

LEARNING AS WE GO ALONG

The President asked the Panel to use the best available scientific research to advise on improvements in the mathematics education of the nation's children, and we have delivered here on his request. Our consistent respect for sound research has been the main factor enabling the Panel's joint conclusions on so many matters, despite differences of perspective and philosophy.

However, we also found no research or insufficient research relating to a great many matters of concern in education policy and practice related to mathematics. In those areas, the Panel has been very limited in what it can report to the President, to the Secretary, and to the public.

A small number of questions have been deemed to have such currency as to require comment from the Panel, even if the scientific evidence was not sufficient to justify research-based findings. In those instances, the Panel has spoken on the basis of collective professional judgment, but it has also endeavored to minimize both the number and the scope of such comments.

The United States has been in a similar situation with respect to education concerns at least once before. When the country was jarred by the challenge of Sputnik, its people responded, in essence, "We see clearly what is broken (math-science education and research), and we are going to fix it by taking the best first steps we can, and then by learning as we go along." And America did. The nation moved rapidly from the doubt of October 1957 into an extended era of achievement and leadership in science and engineering.

The Panel lays out many concrete steps that can be taken now toward significantly improved mathematics education, but it also views them only as a best start in a long process. This journey, like that of the post-Sputnik era, will require a commitment to "learning as we go along." The nation should recognize that there is much more to discover about how to achieve better results. Models of continuous improvement have proven themselves in many other areas, and they can work again for America in mathematics education.

In: Success in Mathematics Education
Editor: Caroline B. Baumann

ISBN: 978-1-60692-299-6
© 2009 Nova Science Publishers, Inc.

Chapter 4

CURRICULAR CONTENT

United States Department of Education

THE NATURE OF SCHOOL ALGEBRA

To clarify instructional needs in Grades K–8 and to sharpen future discussion about the role of school algebra in the overall mathematics curriculum,[1] the Panel made a specific effort to delineate the content and demands of *school algebra*, which is the term used here to encompass the full body of algebraic material that the Panel expects to be covered through high school, regardless of its organization into courses and levels. Most commonly, school algebra is organized into two courses, Algebra I and II. Less commonly, the content of school algebra is interwoven with that of geometry, trigonometry, statistics, and other mathematical subjects in an *integrated curriculum* covering several courses in high school. Even when the traditional pattern of Algebra I and II is used, the course called Algebra II may include elements of statistics or trigonometry in place of some of the more advanced elements of school algebra, which may be offered in a subsequent precalculus course. When the Panel addressed the effective preparation of students for the study of Algebra, its expectation was that students should be able to proceed successfully at least through the content of Algebra II, wherever the elements might be taught in the high school curriculum.

Consequently, the Panel reviewed the algebra topics addressed 1) in current state standards for Algebra I and Algebra II courses and for integrated curricula, 2) in current textbooks for school algebra and integrated mathematics, 3) in the algebra objectives in NAEP's 2005 Grade 12 mathematics assessment, 4) in the

American Diploma Project's benchmarks for a high school exit test and its forthcoming Algebra II end-of-course test, and 5) in the algebra standards in Singapore's mathematics curriculum for Grades 7–10. With professional judgment advised by these comparisons, the Panel sets out the Major Topics of School Algebra, shown in Table 1, as central for the teaching of algebra.[2]

Recommendation: **The Panel recommends that school algebra be consistently understood in terms of the Major Topics of School Algebra given in Table 1.**

Recommendation: **The Major Topics of School Algebra, accompanied by a thorough elucidation of the mathematical connections among these topics,[3] should be the focus of Algebra I and Algebra II standards in state curriculum frameworks, in Algebra I and Algebra II courses, in textbooks for these two levels of Algebra whether for integrated curricula or otherwise, and in end-of-course assessments of these two levels of Algebra. The Panel also recommends use of the Major Topics of School Algebra in revisions of mathematics standards at the high school level in state curriculum frameworks, in high school textbooks organized by an integrated approach, and in grade-level state assessments using an integrated approach at the high school, by Grade 11 at the latest.**

CRITICAL FOUNDATIONS OF ALGEBRA

The mathematics that children learn from preschool through the middle grades provides the basic foundation for Algebra. What is taught at particular grades is determined at local and state levels, and reflects the interests of a variety of national, state, and local agencies and organizations, as well as parents and the general public. In the past, there has been no research base to guide them. However, the results of TIMSS and other international tests showing student achievement across the participating countries have led to international comparisons of curricula and provided much information on what high-achieving countries teach their students in elementary and middle school.

To suggest what essential concepts and skills should be learned as preparation for algebra course work, the Panel reviewed the skills and concepts listed in 1) the Grades 1–8 curricula of the highest-performing countries on TIMSS (Singapore, Japan, Korea, Hong Kong, Flemish Belgium, and the Czech Republic), sometimes called the "A+ countries," 2) National Council of Teachers of Mathematics *Curriculum Focal Points for Prekindergarten through Grade 8 Mathematics: A Quest for Coherence* (hereinafter *Focal Points*), 3) Grades K–8 in the six highest-rated state curriculum frameworks in mathematics, 4) a 2007 American College Testing (ACT) survey, and 5) a Panel-sponsored survey of 743 teachers of introductory Algebra across the country who were asked what students need to learn to be prepared for success in Algebra.

The Panel also took into consideration the structure of mathematics itself, which requires teaching a sequence of major topics (from whole numbers to fractions, from positive numbers to negative numbers, and from the arithmetic of rational numbers to algebra) and an increasingly complex progression from specific number computations to symbolic computations. The structural reasons for this sequence and its increasing complexity dictate what must be taught and learned before students take course work in Algebra.

Based on all these considerations, the Panel proposes three clusters of concepts and skills—called the Critical Foundation of Algebra—reflecting their judgment about the most essential mathematics for students to learn thoroughly prior to algebra course work.

1. ***Fluency with Whole Numbers.*** By the end of Grade 5 or 6, children should have a robust sense of number. This sense of number must include an understanding of place value and the ability to compose and decompose whole numbers. It must clearly include a grasp of the meaning of the basic operations of addition, subtraction, multiplication, and division. It must also include use of the commutative, associative, and distributive properties; computational facility; and the knowledge of how to apply the operations to problem solving. Computational facility requires the automatic recall of addition and related subtraction facts, and of multiplication and related division facts. It also requires fluency with the standard algorithms for addition, subtraction, multiplication, and division. Fluent use of the algorithms not only depends on the automatic recall of number facts but also reinforces it. A strong sense of number also includes the ability to estimate the results of computations and thereby to estimate orders of magnitude, e.g., how many people fit into a stadium or how many gallons of water are needed to fill a pool.

2. ***Fluency with Fractions.*** Before they begin algebra course work, middle school students should have a thorough understanding of positive as well as negative fractions. They should be able to locate positive and negative fractions on a number line; represent and compare fractions, decimals, and related percent; and estimate their size. They need to know that sums, differences, products, and quotients (with nonzero denominators) of fractions are fractions, and they need to be able to carry out these operations confidently and efficiently. They should understand why and how (finite) decimal numbers are fractions and know the meaning of percent. They should encounter fractions in problems in the many contexts in which they arise naturally, for example, to describe rates, proportionality, and probability. Beyond computational facility with specific numbers, the subject of fractions, when properly taught, introduces students to the use of symbolic notation and the concept of generality, both being integral parts of algebra.

3. ***Particular Aspects of Geometry and Measurement.*** Middle grade experience with similar triangles is most directly relevant for the study of Algebra: Sound treatments of the slope of a straight line and of linear functions depend logically on the properties of similar triangles. Furthermore, students should be able to analyze the properties of two- and three-dimensional shapes using formulas to determine perimeter, area, volume, and surface area. They should also be able to find unknown lengths, angles, and areas.

Recommendation: **Proficiency with whole numbers, fractions, and particular aspects of geometry and measurement should be understood as the Critical Foundations of Algebra. Emphasis on these essential concepts and skills must be provided at the elementary and middle grade levels.**

Recommendation: **The coherence and sequential nature of mathematics dictate the foundational skills that are necessary for the learning of algebra. The most important foundational skill not presently developed appears to be proficiency with fractions (including decimals, percent, and negative fractions). The teaching of fractions must be acknowledged as critically important and improved**

before an increase in student achievement in algebra can be expected.

Table 1. The Major Topics of School Algebra

Symbols and Expressions
• Polynomial expressions
• Rational expressions
• Arithmetic and finite geometric series
Linear Equations
• Real numbers as points on the number line
• Linear equations and their graphs
• Solving problems with linear equations
• Linear inequalities and their graphs
• Graphing and solving systems of simultaneous linear equations
Quadratic Equations
• Factors and factoring of quadratic polynomials with integer coefficients
• Completing the square in quadratic expressions
• Quadratic formula and factoring of general quadratic polynomials
• Using the quadratic formula to solve equations
Functions
• Linear functions
• Quadratic functions—word problems involving quadratic functions
• Graphs of quadratic functions and completing the square
• Polynomial functions (including graphs of basic functions)
• Simple nonlinear functions (e.g., square and cube root functions; absolute value; rational functions; step functions)
• Rational exponents, radical expressions, and exponential functions
• Logarithmic functions
• Trigonometric functions
• Fitting simple mathematical models to data
Algebra of Polynomials
• Roots and factorization of polynomials
• Complex numbers and operations
• Fundamental theorem of algebra
• Binomial coefficients (and Pascal's Triangle)
• Mathematical induction and the binomial theorem
Combinatorics and Finite Probability
• Combinations and permutations, as applications of the binomial theorem and Pascal's Triangle.

To prepare students for Algebra, the curriculum must simultaneously develop conceptual understanding, computational fluency, and problem-solving skills. These three aspects of learning are mutually reinforcing and should not be seen as competing for class time.

The Critical Foundations of Algebra identified and discussed here *are not meant to comprise a complete preschool-to-algebra curriculum.* However, the Panel aims to recognize the Critical Foundations of Algebra, whether as part of a dedicated algebra course in Grade 7, 8, or 9, or within an integrated mathematics sequence in the middle and high school grades. These Critical Foundations of Algebra *deserve ample time in any mathematics curriculum.*

Recommendation: **Teacher education programs and licensure tests for early childhood teachers, including all special education teachers at this level, should fully address the topics on whole numbers, fractions, and the appropriate geometry and measurement topics in the Critical Foundations of Algebra, as well as the concepts and skills leading to them; for elementary teachers, including elementary level special education teachers, all topics in the Critical Foundations of Algebra and those topics typically covered in an introductory Algebra course; and for middle school teachers, including middle school special education teachers, the Critical Foundations of Algebra and all of the Major Topics of School Algebra.**

BENCHMARKS FOR THE CRITICAL FOUNDATIONS

In view of the sequential nature of mathematics, the Critical Foundations of Algebra described in the preceding section require judicious placement in the grades leading up to Algebra. To encourage the development of students in Grades PreK–8 at an effective pace, the Panel suggests the Benchmarks for the Critical Foundations in Table 2 as guideposts for state frameworks and school districts. There is no empirical research on the placement of these benchmarks, but they find justification in a comparison of national and international curricula.

Table 2. Benchmarks for the Critical Foundations

	Fluency with Whole Numbers
1.	By the end of Grade 3, students should be proficient with the addition and subtraction of whole numbers.
2.	By the end of Grade 5, students should be proficient with multiplication and division of whole numbers.
	Fluency with Fractions
1.	By the end of Grade 4, students should be able to identify and represent fractions and decimals, and compare them on a number line or with other common representations of fractions and decimals.
2.	By the end of Grade 5, students should be proficient with comparing fractions and decim-als and common percent, and with the addition and subtraction of fractions and decimals.
3.	By the end of Grade 6, students should be proficient with multiplication and division of fractions and decimals.
4.	By the end of Grade 6, students should be proficient with all operations involving posi-tive and negative integers.
5.	By the end of Grade 7, students should be proficient with all operations involving positive and negative fractions.
6.	By the end of Grade 7, students should be able to solve problems involving percent, ratio, and rate and extend this work to proportionality.
	Geometry and Measurement
1.	By the end of Grade 5, students should be able to solve problems involving perimeter and area of triangles and all quadrilaterals having at least one pair of parallel sides (i.e., trapezoids).
2.	By the end of Grade 6, students should be able to analyze the properties of two-dimen-sional shapes and solve problems involving perimeter and area, and analyze the proper-ties of three-dimensional shapes and solve problems involving surface area and volume.
3.	By the end of Grade 7, students should be familiar with the relationship between similar triangles and the concept of the slope of a line.

Recommendation: **The Benchmarks for the Critical Foundations in Table 2 should be used to guide classroom curricula, mathematics instruction, and state assessments. They should be interpreted flexibly, to allow for the needs of students and teachers.**

A NEED FOR COHERENCE

There seem to be two major differences between the curricula in top-performing countries and those in the U.S.—in the number of mathematical concepts or topics presented at each grade level and in the expectations for learning. U.S. curricula typically include many topics at each grade level, with each receiving relatively limited development, while top-performing countries present fewer topics at each grade level but in greater depth. In addition, U.S. curricula generally review and extend at successive grade levels many (if not most) topics already presented at earlier grade levels, while the top-performing countries are more likely to expect closure after exposure, development, and refinement of a particular topic. These critical differences distinguish a spiral curriculum (common in many subjects in U.S. curricula) from one built on developing proficiency—a curriculum that expects proficiency in the topics that are presented before more complex or difficult topics are introduced.

The Singapore standards (Singapore Ministry of Education, 2006) provide an established example of curriculum standards designed to develop proficiency in a relatively small number of important mathematics topics, as validated by a recent analysis (Ginsburg et al., 2005). The desirability of emphasizing fewer important mathematics topics in greater depth has also been recognized by some U.S. educators.

In 2005, the Fordham Foundation report on state mathematics standards (Klein et al., 2005) ranked state mathematics curriculum standards based on mathematics content, clarity, and reasoning, as well as negative qualities, assigning different weights to each criterion for the overall assessment. The standards of California, Indiana, Massachusetts, Alabama, New Mexico, and Georgia achieved the highest ranking. The curricular profiles of the standards of these six states do, on the whole, provide an emphasis on fewer important topics per year than most states; but compared with the "A+ countries" (Singapore, Japan, Korea, Hong Kong, Flemish Belgium, and the Czech Republic), they all spend a great deal of time in the primary grades on topics other than arithmetic.

A more recent development in the national discussion is the publication of *Focal Points* (National Council of Teachers of Mathematics, 2006), which offers curricular direction to teachers and administrators by suggesting areas of emphasis for the concepts, skills, and procedures that connect important mathematics topics from grade to grade, and form the foundation for more advanced mathematics, beginning with Algebra. The message of *Focal Points* is also one of curriculum coherence with an emphasis on fewer important topics per year. *Focal Points* does not represent a set of standards but calls for a curriculum which reduces the number of important topics per year. In effect, *Focal Points* asks for greater emphasis on key topics, particularly with whole numbers and fractions and particular aspects of geometry and measurement. Yet *Focal Points* still implies more time on non-number topics, especially in the primary grades, than is the case in the A+ countries but less than the intended mathematics curriculum as represented in the frameworks of the six states.

The Panel also notes that a state's (or a country's) mathematics standards, however highly their quality may be judged, cannot ensure high student achievement. For example, the six leading states in the Fordham study exhibit a wide range of student achievement on the 2007 NAEP mathematics tests for Grades 4 and 8. The quality of a state's assessments and the extent to which its standards drive sound school curricula, as well as appropriate programs for teacher preparation and professional development, are intervening variables that strongly influence achievement. They may well override the quality of the standards.

> **Recommendation: A focused, coherent progression of mathematics learning, with an emphasis on proficiency with key topics, should become the norm in elementary and middle school mathematics curricula. Any approach that continually revisits topics year after year without closure is to be avoided.**

By the term *focused*, the Panel means that the curriculum must include (and engage with adequate depth in) the most important topics underlying success in school algebra, particularly the Critical Foundations of Algebra. By the term *coherent*, the Panel means that the curriculum is marked by effective, logical progressions from earlier, less sophisticated topics into later, more sophisticated ones.

By the term *proficiency*, the Panel means that students should understand key concepts, achieve automaticity as appropriate (e.g., with addition and related subtraction facts), develop flexible, accurate, and automatic execution of the standard algorithms, and use these competencies to solve problems.[4]

INTEGRATED VERSUS SINGLE-SUBJECT APPROACH

An *integrated approach* is defined as one in which the topics of high school mathematics are presented in some order other than the customary sequence in the United States of yearlong courses in Algebra I, Geometry, Algebra II, and Precalculus.

The curricula of most high-achieving nations in the TIMSS study do not follow the single-subject sequence of Algebra I, Geometry, and Algebra II, but they also differ from the approach used in most U.S. integrated curricula. Instead, Algebra, Geometry, and Trigonometry are divided into blocks. The teaching of each block typically extends over several months and aims for mathematical closure. As a result, these curricula avoid the need to revisit essentially the same material over several years, often referred to as "spiraling."

A search of the literature did not produce studies that clearly examined whether an integrated approach or a single-subject sequence is more effective for algebra and more advanced mathematics course work. The Panel finds no basis in research for preferring one or the other.

An analysis of high school mathematics standards, and one state's standards in particular, suggests that high school students enrolled in mathematics courses using an integrated approach to mathematics may find it more difficult to take advanced mathematics course work (e.g., calculus or precalculus) in their senior year than high school students who are able to enroll in an Algebra II course in their sophomore or junior year.

UNIVERSAL AVAILABILITY OF AUTHENTIC EDUCATION IN ALGEBRA

Recommendation: **All school districts should ensure that all prepared students have access to an authentic algebra course— and should prepare more students than at present to enroll in such a course by Grade 8. The word "authentic" is used here as a descriptor of a course that addresses algebra consistently with the Major Topics of School Algebra (Table 1, page 16). Students must be prepared with the mathematical prerequisites for this course according to the Critical Foundations of Algebra (page 17) and the**

Benchmarks for the Critical Foundations (Table 2, page 20).

End Notes

[1] The detailed work underlying this section was carried out by the Task Group on Conceptual Knowledge and Skills, whose report carries relevant references and more elaborate discussion (National Mathematics Advisory Panel, 2008).

[2] The list of Major Topics of School Algebra is meant as a catalog for coverage, not as a template for how courses should be sequenced or texts should be written.

[3] As presented, for example, in National Mathematics Advisory Panel (2008).

[4] This meaning is in keeping with *Adding It Up* (National Research Council, p. 116), in which five attributes were associated with the concept of proficiency: 1) conceptual understanding (comprehension of mathematical concepts, operations, and relations), 2) procedural fluency (skills in carrying out procedures flexibly, fluently, and appropriately), 3) strategic competence (ability to formulate, represent, and solve mathematical problems), 4) adaptive reasoning (capacity for logical thought, reflection, explanation, and justification), and 5) productive disposition (habitual inclination to see mathematics as sensible, useful, and worthwhile, coupled with a belief in diligence and one's own efficacy).

In: Success in Mathematics Education
Editor: Caroline B. Baumann

ISBN: 978-1-60692-299-6
© 2009 Nova Science Publishers, Inc.

Chapter 5

LEARNING PROCESSES

United States Department of Education

READINESS FOR LEARNING

The mathematics that children learn from preschool through the middle grades provides the basic foundation for Algebra and more advanced mathematics course work.[1] Even before they enter kindergarten, most children develop considerable knowledge of numbers and other aspects of mathematics. The mathematical knowledge that children bring to school influences their math learning for many years thereafter, and probably throughout their education.

When they enter kindergarten, most children from families with the combination of low-parental education levels, low incomes, and single parents bring less foundational knowledge for learning school mathematics than does the average child from more advantaged backgrounds. Fortunately, a variety of promising instructional programs have been developed to improve the mathematical knowledge of preschoolers and kindergartners, especially those from at-risk backgrounds, and have yielded encouraging results.

Recommendation: **Research that scales up early interventions capable of strengthening mathematical knowledge, evaluates their utility in prekindergarten and kindergarten settings, and examines long-term effects are urgently needed, with a particular focus on at-risk learners.**

Recommendation: **Teachers in Head Start and other programs serving preschoolers from low-income backgrounds should be made aware of the importance of early mathematical knowledge for long-term educational success and of the availability of effective techniques for improving that knowledge. Training in how to implement these teaching techniques must be included in the intervention studies carried out pursuant to the above recommendation and should be made available to interested teachers and preschools.**

WHOLE NUMBER ARITHMETIC: COMPUTATIONAL PROFICIENCY PLUS CONCEPTUAL UNDERSTANDING

Debates regarding the relative importance of conceptual knowledge, procedural skills (e.g., the standard algorithms), and the commitment of addition, subtraction, multiplication, and division facts to long-term memory are misguided. These capabilities are mutually supportive, each facilitating learning of the others. Conceptual understanding of mathematical operations, fluent execution of procedures, and fast access to number combinations together support effective and efficient problem solving.

Computational facility with whole number operations rests on the automatic recall of addition and related subtraction facts, and of multiplication and related division facts. It requires fluency with the standard algorithms for addition, subtraction, multiplication, and division. Fluent use of the algorithms not only depends on the automatic recall of number facts but also reinforces it.

Studies of children in the United States, comparisons of these children with children from other nations with higher mathematics achievement, and even cross-generational changes within the United States indicate that many contemporary U.S. children do not reach the point of fast and efficient solving of single-digit addition, subtraction, multiplication, and division with whole numbers, much less fluent execution of more complex algorithms as early as children in many other countries. Surprisingly, many never gain such proficiency.

The reasons for differences in the computational fluency of children in the United States and peers in countries with higher mathematics achievement are multifaceted. They include quantity and quality of practice, emphases within curricula, and parental involvement in mathematics learning. As an example, in elementary school textbooks in the United States, easier arithmetic problems are presented far more frequently than harder problems. The opposite is the case in countries with higher mathematics achievement, such as Singapore.

Few curricula in the United States provide sufficient practice to ensure fast and efficient solving of basic fact combinations and execution of the standard algorithms.

Too many American students also have a poor grasp of many core arithmetical concepts. For example, many U.S. middle school students do not understand the concept of mathematical equality. Understanding core concepts is a necessary component of proficiency with arithmetic and is needed to transfer previously learned procedures to solve novel problems. U.S. students' poor knowledge of the core arithmetical concepts impedes their learning of algebra and is an unacceptable indication of a substantive gap in the mathematics curricula that must be addressed.

NUMBER SENSE

In its most fundamental form, number sense entails an ability to immediately identify the numerical value associated with small quantities (e.g., 3 pennies), a facility with basic counting skills, and a proficiency in approximating the magnitudes of small numbers of objects and simple numerical operations. An intuitive sense of the magnitudes of small whole numbers is evident even among most 5-year-olds who can, for example, accurately judge which of two single digits is larger, estimate the number of dots on a page, and determine the approximate location of single digit numerals on a number line that provides only the numerical endpoints. These competencies comprise the core number sense that children often acquire informally prior to starting school.

A more advanced type of number sense that children must acquire through formal instruction requires a principled understanding of place value, of how whole numbers can be composed and decomposed, and of the meaning of the basic arithmetic operations of addition, subtraction, multiplication, and division. It also requires understanding the commutative, associative, and distributive properties and knowing how to apply these principles to solve problems. This more highly developed form of number sense should extend to numbers written in fraction, decimal, percent, and exponential forms. Far too many middle and high school students lack the ability to accurately compare the magnitudes of such numbers. This is a serious problem, because poor number sense interferes with learning algorithms and number facts and prevents use of strategies to verify if solutions to problems are reasonable. Analysis of the literature on number sense suggests two specific recommendations:

Recommendation: **Teachers should broaden instruction in computational estimation beyond rounding. They should ensure that students understand that the purpose of estimation is to approximate the exact value and that rounding is only one estimation strategy.**

Recommendation: **Textbooks need to explicitly explain that the purpose of estimation is to produce an appropriate approximation. Illustrating multiple useful estimation strategies for a single problem, and explaining how each procedure achieves the goal of an appropriate estimate, is a useful means for achieving this goal. Contrasting these procedures with others that produce less appropriate estimates is also likely to be helpful.**

FRACTIONS

Difficulty with the learning of fractions is pervasive and is an obstacle to further progress in mathematics and other domains dependent on mathematics, including algebra. It also has been linked to difficulties in adulthood, such as failure to understand medication regimens. Algebra I teachers who were surveyed for the Panel as part of a large, nationally representative sample rated students as having very poor preparation in "rational numbers and operations involving fractions and decimals" (see Panel-commissioned National Survey of Algebra Teachers, National Mathematics Advisory Panel, 2008).

Preschool and early elementary school children have a rudimentary understanding of simple fractional relations. The relation between this informal knowledge and the learning of formal mathematical fractional concepts and procedures is not well understood, and is an area in critical need of further study.

Elementary and middle school children should begin fraction instruction with the prerequisite ability to quickly and easily retrieve basic arithmetic facts, execute arithmetic procedures involving whole numbers, and deeply understand core concepts involving whole numbers. Teachers should not assume that children understand the magnitudes represented by fractions, even if the children can perform arithmetic operations with them, or that children understand what the operations mean (e.g., understand what it means to multiply or divide one fraction by another). Instruction focusing on conceptual knowledge of fractions is likely to have the broadest and largest impact on problem-solving performance, provided it is aimed at accurately solving problems that tap conceptual knowledge. Procedural knowledge is also essential and is likely to enhance conceptual knowledge and vice versa.

Studies in the scientific literature reveal features of children's understanding of fractions that should be transferable to their learning in classrooms. These potential interventions include using fraction names that demarcate parts and wholes and linking common fraction representations to locations on number lines. Conceptual and procedural knowledge about fractions with magnitudes less than 1 do not necessarily transfer to fractions with magnitudes greater than 1. Therefore, understanding of fractions with magnitudes in each range needs to be taught directly, and the relation between them needs to be discussed.

As with learning whole numbers, conceptual and procedural knowledge of fractions reinforce one another and influence such varied tasks as estimation, computation, and the solution of word problems. One key mechanism linking conceptual and procedural knowledge is the ability to represent fractions on a number line.

> **Recommendation:** **The curriculum should allow for sufficient time to ensure acquisition of conceptual and procedural knowledge of fractions (including decimals and percent) and of proportional reasoning. The curriculum should include representational supports that have been shown to be effective, such as number line representations, and should encompass instruction in tasks that tap the full gamut of conceptual and procedural knowledge, including ordering fractions on a number line, judging equivalence and relative magnitudes of fractions with unlike numerators and denominators, and solving problems involving ratios and proportion.**

The curriculum also should make explicit
connections between intuitive understanding and
formal problem solving involving fractions.

Recommendation: Research is needed on how children can be taught to
appropriately estimate the magnitudes of fractions
and on how learning to estimate those magnitudes
influences acquisition of other skills involving
fractions, such as arithmetic and algebra.

GEOMETRY AND MEASUREMENT

Although early exposure to basic geometric shapes, names, and other
concepts may be helpful in developing children's formal geometric knowledge
and skills, this is not sufficient. Despite the widespread use of mathematical
manipulatives such as geoboards and dynamic software, evidence regarding their
usefulness in helping children learn geometry is tenuous at best. Students must
eventually transition from concrete (hands-on) or visual representations to
internalized abstract representations. The crucial steps in making such transitions
are not clearly understood at present and need to be a focus of learning and
curriculum research.

Recommendation: Teachers should recognize that from early childhood
through the elementary school years, the spatial
visualization skills needed for learning geometry
have already begun to develop. In contrast to the
claims of Piagetian theory, young children appear to
possess at least an implicit understanding of basic
facets of Euclidean concepts. However, formal
instruction is necessary to ensure that children build
upon this knowledge to learn geometry.

GENERAL PRINCIPLES OF LEARNING

Students learn by building on prior knowledge, extending as far back as early
childhood. Learning and development are incremental processes that occur

gradually and continuously over many years. Even during the preschool period, children have considerably greater reasoning and problem-solving ability than was suspected until recently.

For all content areas, conceptual understanding, computational fluency, and problem-solving skills are each essential and mutually reinforcing, influencing performance on such varied tasks as estimation, word problems, and computation.

For all content areas, practice allows students to achieve automaticity of basic skills—the fast, accurate, and effortless processing of content information—which frees up working memory for more complex aspects of problem solving. The issue of transfer, that is, the ability to use skills learned to solve one class of problems, such as similar triangles, to solve another class of problems, such as linear algebra, is a vital part of mathematics learning. Of particular importance is determining the variables that impede or facilitate transfer. Studies of transfer suggest that people's ability to make links between related domains is limited; studies on how to foster transfer in key mathematical domains are needed.

Teachers and developers of instructional materials sometimes assume that students need to be a certain age to learn certain mathematical ideas. However, a major finding, documented in a National Research Council synthesis of studies about science learning and reaffirmed in the review of learning studies in mathematics conducted by the Task Group on Learning Processes, is, "What is developmentally appropriate is not a simple function of age or grade, but rather is largely contingent on prior opportunities to learn" (Duschl et al., 2007, p. 2). Claims based on Piaget's highly influential theory, and related theories of "developmental appropriateness" that children of particular ages cannot learn certain content because they are "too young," "not in the appropriate stage," or "not ready" have consistently been shown to be wrong. Nor are claims justified that children cannot learn particular ideas because their brains are insufficiently developed, even if they possess the prerequisite knowledge for learning the ideas.

The sociocultural perspective of Vygotsky has also been influential in education. It characterizes learning as a social induction process through which learners become increasingly independent through the tutelage of more knowledgeable peers and adults. However, its utility in mathematics classrooms and mathematics curricula remains to be scientifically tested.

SOCIAL, MOTIVATIONAL AND AFFECTIVE INFLUENCES

Understanding how children gain proficiency in mathematics requires more than knowledge about how they learn in content areas. Children's goals and beliefs about learning are also critical.

Children who seek to master an academic topic are said to have mastery-oriented goals. These children show better long-term academic development in mathematics than do their peers whose main goals are to get good grades or outperform others. Students who believe learning mathematics is strongly related to innate ability show less persistence on complex tasks than peers who believe that effort is more important.

Experimental studies have demonstrated that children's beliefs about the relative importance of effort and ability or inherent talent can be changed, and that increased emphasis on the importance of effort is related to greater engagement in mathematics learning and, through this engagement, improved mathematics grades and achievement.

Research demonstrating that beliefs about effort matter and that these beliefs can be changed is critical. Much of the public's resignation about mathematics education (together with the common tendencies to dismiss weak achievement and to give up early) seems rooted in the idea that success in mathematics is largely a matter of inherent talent, not effort.

Recommendation: The Panel recommends that teachers and other educational leaders use research-based interventions to help students and parents understand the vital importance of effort in learning mathematics.

Anxiety about mathematics performance is related to low mathematics grades, failure to enroll in advanced mathematics courses, and poor scores on standardized tests of mathematics achievement. It also may be related to failure to graduate from high school. At present, however, little is known about its onset or the factors responsible for it. Potential risk factors for mathematics anxiety include low mathematics aptitude, low working memory capacity, vulnerability to public embarrassment, and negative teacher and parent attitudes.

Recommendation: **The Panel recommends research that assesses potential risk factors for mathematics anxiety; it also recommends development of promising interventions for reducing serious mathematics anxiety.**

Mathematics performance and learning of groups that have traditionally been underrepresented in mathematics fields can be considerably improved by interventions that address social, affective, and motivational factors. Recent research documents that social and intellectual support from peers and teachers is associated with higher mathematics performance for all students, and that such support is especially important for many African-American and Hispanic students.

Recommendation: **The Panel recommends the scaling-up and experimental evaluation of support-focused interventions that have been shown to improve the mathematics outcomes of African-American and Hispanic students. These and related studies focused on improving task engagement and self-efficacy of such students hold promise for helping to close the mathematics achievement gaps that are prevalent in U.S. society.**

Average gender differences are small or nonexistent, and our society's focus on them has diverted attention from the essential task of raising the scores of both boys and girls.

Progress has been made in understanding the difficulties that children with learning disabilities have with the learning of concepts, procedures, and facts in some areas of arithmetic. However, little is known about the source of their difficulties in other core areas, including fractions and algebra. Preliminary research has identified some of the mechanisms that contribute to exceptional mathematics learning, but much remains to be discovered.

Recommendation: **Research on the cognitive mechanisms that contribute to learning disabilities and precocious learning in mathematical domains beyond whole number arithmetic is needed to better understand the sources of individual differences in children's mathematical learning.**

CONSIDERATIONS SPECIFIC TO ALGEBRA

There are many gaps in the current understanding of how students learn algebra and the preparation that is needed before they enter Algebra. What is known indicates that too many students in middle or high school algebra classes are woefully unprepared for learning even the basics of algebra. The types of errors these students make when attempting to solve algebraic equations reveal they do not have a firm understanding of many basic principles of arithmetic. Many students also have difficulty grasping the syntax or structure of algebraic expressions and do not understand procedures for transforming equations or why transformations are done the way they are. These and other difficulties are compounded as equations become more complex and when students attempt to solve word problems.

Algebra teachers should not assume that all students understand even basic concepts, such as mathematical equality. Many students will not have a sufficient understanding of the commutative and distributive properties, for example, to take full advantage of instruction in algebra. Many students will need extensive practice at solving algebraic equations and explanation as to why the equations are solved in a particular way—for instance, to maintain equality across the two sides of an equation. Examining common errors with students may provide an opportunity to discuss and remediate overgeneralizations or misconceptions.

Recommendation: **Longitudinal research is needed to identify early predictors of success or failure in algebra. The identification of these predictors will help to guide the design of interventions that will build the foundational skills needed for success in algebra.**

End Notes

[1] The detailed work underlying this section was carried out by the Task Group on Learning Processes, whose report carries relevant references and more elaborate discussion (National Mathematics Advisory Panel, 2008).

In: Success in Mathematics Education
Editor: Caroline B. Baumann

ISBN: 978-1-60692-299-6
© 2009 Nova Science Publishers, Inc.

Chapter 6

TEACHERS AND TEACHER EDUCATION

United States Department of Education

Substantial differences in mathematics achievement of students are attributable to differences in teachers.[1] Teachers are crucial to students' opportunities to learn and to their learning of mathematics.

There are large, measurable differences in the effectiveness of mathematics teachers in generating achievement gains:

- Differences in teachers account for 12% to 14% of total variability in students' mathematics achievement gains during an elementary school year.
- When teachers are ranked according to their ability to produce student achievement gains, there is a 10 percentile point difference across the course of a school year between achievement gains of students of top-quartile teachers versus bottom-quartile teachers.
- The effects of teachers on student achievement compound dramatically if students receive a series of effective or ineffective teachers.

Vital, therefore, to the Panel's inquiry and recommendations is the best available evidence on how teachers' own knowledge matters for students' achievement and how effective teachers can be best recruited, prepared, supported, and rewarded. The Panel found an uneven research base to address these questions.

TEACHERS' MATHEMATICAL KNOWLEDGE

Teachers' mathematical knowledge was estimated in three different ways across the research we reviewed: certification, courses completed, and direct tests of teachers' knowledge of mathematics. The Panel appraised what is known about the relationships between teachers' content knowledge, as measured in each of these ways, and students' achievement.

Teacher Certification as a Measure of Mathematical Knowledge

Overall, findings about the relationship between teacher certification (i.e., licensure) and student achievement in mathematics have been mixed, even among the most rigorous and highest-quality studies. Research in this area has not provided consistent or convincing evidence that students of teachers who are certified to teach mathematics gain more than those whose teachers are not. The relationship between teacher certification status, the most inexact proxy for teachers' content knowledge, and students' mathematics achievement remains ambiguous.

Content Course Work and Degrees as Measures of Mathematical Knowledge

Studies that used the mathematics courses that teachers have taken as a proxy for their mathematical knowledge showed mixed results regarding the relationship of teachers' content knowledge to their students' achievement at the elementary and middle school level. At the secondary school level, there appears to be some effect of teachers' content knowledge when it is measured in terms of teachers' course-taking. However, the available evidence does not support this relationship below ninth grade.

Tests and Ad Hoc Assessments as Measures of Mathematical Knowledge

Some studies of practicing teachers at the elementary and middle school level that used tests of specific mathematical knowledge for teaching and other ad hoc measures also yielded mixed results. Overall, however, the evidence suggests a positive relationship between teachers' mathematical knowledge and gains in student achievement. The one study that used test items specifically designed to directly measure the mathematical content knowledge used in teaching did produce findings whose magnitude is substantially larger than the others. Because these studies were focused at the elementary level, comparisons with other findings are difficult.

The inability to draw solid conclusions from this literature is in part due to a historical lack of high-quality measures of mathematics content knowledge, as well as a paucity of high-quality studies using these types of measures.

The Mathematical Content and Nature of Teacher Licensure Exams

Recent research treating teacher licensure as a proxy for teachers' mathematical knowledge has not shown consistently or convincingly that students of teachers who are licensed to teach mathematics gain more academically than those whose teachers are not. However, since the 1998 reauthorization of the *Higher Education Act*, teacher licensure exams have come to play an important role in determining the quality and quantity of teachers available to teach mathematics. Therefore the Panel also attempted to assess the mathematical content covered on teachers' licensure exams and the rigor and relevance of those exams. There are three major developers of teacher licensure tests: The Educational Testing Service (ETS), National Evaluation Systems (NES), and the American Board for Certification of Teacher Excellence (ABCTE). For those states that contract with ETS, prospective teachers take the *Praxis* series, which comprises two separate exams, the Praxis I and II. The Praxis I exams are designed to measure basic skills in reading, writing, and mathematics. Most ETS states currently require the Praxis I tests for licensure, and often for admission into their teacher education programs. The Praxis II exams for those who will teach mathematics as content specialists or as generalists vary in the amount and level of mathematical knowledge assessed. Some of these tests do not assess mathematics content. To analyze the effectiveness of these exams in assessing teachers' content knowledge, the Panel sought access to exams together with data on teachers' performance on each item. Due to issues of confidentiality, however, the Panel was not able to gather sufficiently complete information to assess the mathematical quality of these exams.

Conclusions about the Relationship of Teachers' Mathematical Knowledge to Students' Achievement Gains

Overall, across the studies reviewed by the Panel, it is clear that teachers' knowledge of mathematics is positively related to student achievement. However, evidence about the relationship of elementary and middle school teachers' mathematical knowledge to students' mathematics achievement remains uneven and has been surprisingly difficult to produce. One important reason has been the lack of valid and reliable measures of teachers' mathematical knowledge. The literature has been dominated by the use of proxies for such knowledge, such as certification status and mathematics course work completed. A second reason for the inconsistent findings has been weak study designs. Too few studies exist that set up proper comparisons or use sufficient sample sizes or appropriate analytic methods. Selection bias and failure to isolate potentially important variables from confounding variables have further plagued these studies, as have inadequate measures of students' mathematics achievement. Finally, with the exception of one study that directly measured the mathematical knowledge used in teaching, no studies identified by the Panel probed the dynamic that would examine how elementary and middle school teachers' mathematical knowledge affects instructional quality, students' opportunities to learn, and gains in achievement over time.

In the context of a body of literature as inexact as this one, the positive trends we identified *do* support the importance of teachers' knowledge of mathematics as a factor in students' achievement.

Recommendation: **Teachers must know in detail the mathematical content they are responsible for teaching and its connections to other important mathematics, both prior to and beyond the level they are assigned to teach. However, because most studies have relied on proxies for teachers' mathematical knowledge (e.g., course work as part of a certification program), existing research does not provide definitive evidence for the specific mathematical knowledge and skill that are needed for teaching.**

Recommendation: **More precise measures should be developed to uncover in detail the relationships among teachers' knowledge, their instructional skill, and students'**

learning, and to identify the mathematical and pedagogical knowledge needed for teaching.

Recommendation: The mathematics preparation of elementary and middle school teachers must be strengthened as one means for improving teachers' effectiveness in the classroom. This includes preservice teacher education, early career support, and professional development programs. A critical component of this recommendation is that teachers be given ample opportunities to learn mathematics for teaching. That is, teachers must know in detail and from a more advanced perspective the mathematical content they are responsible for teaching and the connections of that content to other important mathematics, both prior to and beyond the level they are assigned to teach.

High-quality research must be undertaken to create a sound basis for the mathematics preparation of elementary and middle school teachers within preservice teacher education, early-career support, and ongoing professional development programs. Outcomes of different approaches should be evaluated by using reliable and valid measures of their effects on prospective and current teachers' instructional techniques and, most important, their effects on student achievement.

TEACHERS' EDUCATION: PREPARATION, INDUCTION, AND PROFESSIONAL DEVELOPMENT

The Panel investigated evidence on the impact of:

- *Preservice teacher preparation*: Initial teacher training, conventionally offered in institutions of higher education;
- *Alternative pathways*: Initial teacher preparation offered outside of conventional teacher education programs;

- *Induction programs*: Programs of professional support and additional training within the first years of teachers' practice;
- *Professional development*: Ongoing programmatic professional education of practicing teachers.

The focus was on what is known about the relationship between different forms of teacher education and the learning of teachers and their students:

Preservice Teacher Preparation

Very few empirical studies were found that addressed the impacts of preparation programs on student achievement or teachers' mathematical knowledge. Unfortunately, none of these studies was of sufficient rigor or quality to allow the Panel to draw conclusions about the relationship of particular features of teacher preparation programs and their effects.

Alternative Pathways into Teaching

With respect to alternative pathways into teaching, there were a few studies that compared the effectiveness of standard and alternative preparation programs on student achievement, suggesting that there is no basis in research for preferring one pathway to another. The extant evidence suggests that there are not significant differences among current pathways. Moreover, the variation within programs appears to be greater than that found across programs.

Early-Career Teacher Support Programs

No peer-reviewed studies could be found that focused on the effects of programs for first- and second-year mathematics teachers (i.e., induction programs) on student achievement or on teachers' mathematics knowledge. The key outcome for much of the extant induction literature is teacher retention. There also is a wealth of literature examining the qualitative effects of induction programs on teacher beliefs, satisfaction, and practices. Induction programs continue to expand, some with and some without mandated funding. Given the expansion, it is important to assess the effectiveness of induction programs on student achievement as well as on teacher retention.

Professional Development

The Panel searched for peer-reviewed research and national reports that would offer high-quality evidence regarding the impact of professional development programs for teachers, but found that many studies were descriptive. Most of the studies that were intended to be empirical tests of hypotheses did not include a comparison group, but used a "one-group pretest/posttest design." Moreover, many studies relied on teachers' self-reports about their knowledge before and after the professional development rather than on objective measures of teacher knowledge. Consequently, the studies that the Panel was able to include were only ones that examined the relationship between teacher professional development programs and students' mathematics achievement.

Although the Panel did find some positive effects of professional development on students' achievement gains, research does not yield sufficient evidence on the features of any particular approach to permit detailed conclusions about the forms of or approaches to effective professional development.

CONCLUSIONS ABOUT THE IMPACT OF TEACHERS' EDUCATION ON TEACHERS' MATHEMATICAL KNOWLEDGE OR STUDENTS' ACHIEVEMENT GAINS

Despite widespread beliefs about the qualities that make teacher education effective, the Panel did not find strong evidence for the impact of any specific form of, or approach to, teacher education on either teachers' knowledge or students' learning. Even for the few studies that did produce significant effects, little detail was provided about the features of the training that might account for the impact of the program. Such deficiencies of the research impeded the Panel's ability to identify crucial components of teacher education.

Much more needs to be known about features of professional development programs that are able to equip teachers with the knowledge and skills they need to facilitate student learning.

Recommendation: **The Panel recommends that a sharp focus be placed on systematically strengthening teacher preparation, early-career mentoring and support, and ongoing professional development for teachers of mathematics at every level, with special emphasis on ways to ensure appropriate content knowledge for teaching.**

Recommendation: **A well-designed program of research and evaluation, meeting standards permitting the generalization of results, should be undertaken to create a sound basis for the education of teachers of mathematics.**

Key questions on which robust evidence is needed include:

- Does teacher education (including preservice training of different kinds, professional development, and early career induction programs) have an impact on teachers' capacity and on students' achievement?
- What are the key features of teacher education (e.g., duration, structure, quantity, content, pedagogy, structure, relationship to practice) that have effects on teachers' capacity and on students' achievement?
- How do contexts (e.g., school, students, teachers, policy) affect the outcomes of professional development?
- How do different amounts of teacher education affect its outcomes and effects?

Given the vast investment made in teacher education, knowledge about the effectiveness of different approaches is vitally needed. Well-conceived efforts to improve the outcomes of teacher education, to improve measures of those outcomes, and to implement better research strategies should be supported.

RECRUITMENT AND RETENTION STRATEGIES TO ATTRACT AND RETAIN EFFECTIVE TEACHERS OF MATHEMATICS

Because compensation is often cited as a key factor in improving teacher quality, the Panel investigated evidence on how different salary schemes work to recruit, reward, and retain skillful teachers.

In the business sector, pay is typically contingent on performance and area of specialization as well as on years of experience and level of education. In universities, for example, economists typically receive higher salaries than historians, reflecting the greater demand for economists outside academe. Parallels in K–12 education would take the form of paying more to teachers who have technical skills that are in demand in other sectors of the economy, such as teachers with degrees in mathematics (*skills-based pay*), and paying more to mathematics teachers who are more productive in raising student achievement (*performance-based pay*). Another type of incentive has the purpose of compensating teachers for working in conditions they view as unfavorable (*location-based pay*), such as those associated with high-poverty, low-achieving schools. The Panel examined research on each of these approaches to teacher compensation.

Skills-Based Pay

College students' decisions to prepare for and enter into teaching depend on how the salary structure for teachers compares with those in competing occupations. The magnitude of the salary differential between the private sector and the teaching profession for those who enter teaching with technical training is large, with a negligible difference on entry but a rapidly increasing gap over the first 10 years of employment. Teachers of mathematics and science are significantly more likely to leave their teaching jobs because of job dissatisfaction than are other teachers (40% of math and science teachers and 29% of all teachers). Of those mathematics and science teachers who depart because of job dissatisfaction, the most common reason given is low salaries (57% of respondents).

Location-Based Pay

Research on the effects of location-based pay, intended to attract or retain skilled teachers in schools that serve under-resourced communities, yields mixed results. The effectiveness of such salary schemes is affected by the amount of differential in pay, the gender and experience of the teacher, and whether the bonus is a one-time signing bonus or a permanently higher salary, as well as other factors.

Performance-Based Pay

The Panel identified four different aspects of "merit" pay: whether salary differentials are tied to schools' performance or that of individual teachers, how significant the pay differential is, the degree to which the scheme is focused on student performance, and whether the plan seems continuous or is a short-term experiment. Across the studies reviewed, each found some positive effects on student achievement, but none was sufficient to reach strong conclusions about the effectiveness of performance-based pay schemes.

The results from research on teacher incentives generally support the effectiveness of incentives, although the methodological quality of the studies in terms of causal conclusions is mixed. The substantial body of economic research in other fields indicating that salary affects the number of workers entering a field and their job performance is relevant. In the context of the totality of the evidence, and acknowledging the substantial number of unknowns, the NMP recommends policy initiatives that put in place and carefully evaluate the effects of:

- Raising base salaries for teachers of mathematics to attract more mathematically qualified teachers into the workforce;
- Salary incentives for teachers of mathematics for working in locations that are difficult to staff, and;
- Opportunities for teachers of mathematics to increase their base salaries substantially by demonstrable effectiveness in raising student achievement.

Considerable work remains to be done before enough will be known to put particular pay-for-performance systems in place and to confidently predict their outcomes. Knowing more about how various incentive systems affect teachers would enable the design of more effective and efficient incentives. Additional evidence also shows that teachers' decisions to remain in teaching and to continue teaching in particular schools are affected by factors in addition to salary, including work conditions, the proximity of teachers' residences to the school, support from school administrators, teaching assignments, and characteristics of students.

ELEMENTARY MATHEMATICS SPECIALIST TEACHERS

There have been many calls in recent years for the use of "math specialists" at the K–5 level, but what is meant by "math specialists" can take different forms. The Panel sought to learn what is known about such specialists at the elementary level.

Models of Math Specialists

The Panel identified at least three types of "math specialist teachers": the math coach (lead teacher), the full-time elementary mathematics teacher, and the pull-out program teacher. Math coaches are more common than the other two types, but there is considerable blurring across types and roles. *Math coaches* (sometimes called *lead teachers*) tend to act as resources for their colleagues and do not directly instruct students. They work at the state, district, and school levels, providing leadership and information to teachers and staff and often coordinating mathematics programs within a school, a district, or across districts. *Full-time mathematics teacher*s are responsible for the direct instruction of students. They work at the school and district levels, but most frequently take responsibilities in one school. *Pull-out program teachers* represent a variation of the specialized teacher model. In this model, math specialists directly instruct individuals or small groups of students within or outside a regular classroom.

Effects on Student Achievement of Using Math Specialists

Very few studies were identified that probed the effectiveness of elementary mathematics specialists of any of the three types. Out of 114 potentially relevant pieces of literature, only 1 explored the effects of mathematics specialists on student achievement in elementary schools. These authors found no difference in the mathematics gain scores of students in an elementary school with a departmentalized structure compared to students in a school with a self-contained structure.

Costs Associated with Using Math Specialists

One cost has to do with the funding of the personnel involved and depends on the model used. The use of a full-time mathematics teacher involves only a redistribution of responsibilities among the existing staff, whereas the use of math coaches and pull-out teachers requires the hiring of additional staff. A second cost is that of the additional training needed for teachers to gain the specialized knowledge needed to fill these roles.

The Use of Math Specialists in Other Countries

Full-time elementary mathematics teachers are not widely used in most of the countries that produce high levels of student achievement in mathematics. Only three (China, Singapore, and Sweden) deploy such teachers at the elementary level. That elementary teachers in those countries may enter teaching with stronger backgrounds in mathematics may be a factor in the success of those countries with mathematics education.

Recommendation: **The Panel recommends that research be conducted on the use of full-time mathematics teachers in elementary schools. These would be teachers with strong knowledge of mathematics who would teach mathematics full-time to several classrooms of students, rather than teaching many subjects to one class, as is typical in most elementary classrooms. This recommendation for research is based on the Panel's findings about the importance of teachers' mathematical knowledge. The use of teachers who have specialized in elementary mathematics teaching could be a practical alternative to increasing all elementary teachers' content knowledge (a problem of huge scale) by focusing the need for expertise on fewer teachers.**

End Notes

[1] The detailed work underlying this section was carried out by the Task Group on Teachers and Teacher Education, whose report carries relevant references and more elaborate discussion (National Mathematics Advisory Panel, 2008).

In: Success in Mathematics Education
Editor: Caroline B. Baumann

ISBN: 978-1-60692-299-6
© 2009 Nova Science Publishers, Inc.

Chapter 7

INSTRUCTIONAL PRACTICES

United States Department of Education

TEACHER-DIRECTED AND STUDENT-CENTERED INSTRUCTION IN MATHEMATICS

A controversial issue in the field of mathematics education is whether classroom instruction should be more teacher directed or more student centered.[1] These terms encompass a wide array of meanings, with teacher-directed instruction ranging from highly scripted direct instruction approaches to interactive lecture styles, and with student-centered instruction ranging from students having primary responsibility for their own mathematics learning to highly structured cooperative groups. Schools and districts must make choices about curricular materials and instructional approaches that often seem more aligned with one instructional orientation than another. This leaves teachers wondering about when to organize their instruction one way or the other, whether certain topics are taught more effectively with one approach or another, and whether certain students benefit more from one approach than another.

In the Panel's review, the search was limited to studies that directly compared these two extreme positions. We defined teacher-directed instruction as instruction in which it is the teacher who is primarily communicating the mathematics to the students directly and student-centered instruction as instruction in which students are primarily doing the teaching.

We found only eight studies that met our standards for quality and that compared versions of teacher-directed and student-centered instruction consistent with our definition. The studies presented a mixed and inconclusive picture of the relative effect of these two approaches to instruction. Although there were some significant effect sizes in some studies in both groups, all had limitations and no generalizations can be made. Additional high-quality research is needed, using clear definitions of "teacher directed" and "student centered."

> **Recommendation:** **All-encompassing recommendations that instruction should be entirely "student centered" or "teacher directed" are not supported by research. If such recommendations exist, they should be rescinded. If they are being considered, they should be avoided. High-quality research does not support the exclusive use of either approach.**

One of the major shifts in education over the past 25–30 years has been advocacy for the increased use of cooperative learning groups and peer-to-peer learning (e.g., structured activities for students working in pairs) in the teaching and learning of mathematics. Use of cooperative or collaborative learning has been advocated in various mathematics education reports and in state curricular frameworks, policies, and instructional guidelines. Cooperative learning is used for multiple purposes: for tutoring, for enrichment and for remediation, as an occasional substitute for independent seatwork, for intricate extension activities, for initial brainstorming, and for numerous other purposes.

The Panel located high-quality studies in the following areas of cooperative and collaborative learning: Team Assisted Individualization (four studies), Student Teams-Achievement Division (six studies), peer-to-peer learning strategies (five studies), other cooperative learning strategies (five studies), studies combining cooperative learning with other instructional practices (three studies), and studies investigating cooperative learning in the context of computers (eight studies).

Research has been conducted on a variety of cooperative learning approaches. One such approach, Team Assisted Individualization (TAI), has been shown to improve students' computation skills. This highly structured instructional approach involves heterogeneous groups of students helping each other, individualized problems based on student performance on a diagnostic test, specific teacher guidance, and rewards based on both group and individual performance. Effects of TAI on conceptual understanding and problem solving were not significant.

There is suggestive evidence that peer tutoring improves computation skills in the elementary grades. However, additional research is needed.

USING FORMATIVE ASSESSMENT

Formative assessment—the ongoing monitoring of student learning to inform instruction—is generally considered a hallmark of effective instruction in any discipline.

Our key findings from a review of the high-quality studies of this topic are:

- The average gain in learning provided by teachers' use of formative assessments is marginally significant. Results suggest that use of formativeassessments benefited students at all ability levels. When teachers are provided with additional "enhancements" (i.e., specific suggestions on how to use the assessment data to provide differentiated instruction), the pooled effect is significant.
- The studies describe a set of tools and procedures (what are called "enhancements") that can accompany formative assessment. Given the nature of the evidence, the Panel would more cautiously call these practices promising as opposed to evidence-based.
- Only one type of formative assessment has been studied with rigorous experimentation, viz. assessment that includes a random sampling of items that address state standards. The assessments tend to take between two and eight minutes to administer and, thus, are feasible for regular use.

Teachers' regular use of formative assessments improves their students' learning, especially if teachers have additional guidance on using the assessment results to design and individualize instruction. The research to date has only involved formative assessment based on items sampled from the major curriculum objectives for the year as specified by state standards. Findings regarding use of this type of formative assessment were consistently positive and significant.

Recommendation: **Based on its review of research, the Panel recommends   regular   use   of   formative**

assessment, particularly for students in the elementary grades. These assessments need to provide information not only on their content validity but also on their reliability and their criterion-related validity (i.e., correlation of these measures with other measures of mathematics proficiency). For struggling students, frequent (e.g., weekly or biweekly) use of these assessments appears optimal, so that instruction can be adapted based on student progress.

Although the research base is smaller, and less consistent than that on the general effectiveness of formative assessment, the research does suggest that several specific tools and strategies can help teachers use formative assessment information more effectively. The first promising strategy is providing formative assessment information to teachers (via technology) on content and concepts that require additional work with the whole class. The second promising strategy involves using technology to specify activities needed by individual students. Both of these aids can be implemented via tutoring, computer-assisted instruction, or help provided by a professional (teacher, mathematics specialist, trained paraprofessional).

Recommendation: The Panel recommends that professional organizations, school districts, and state agencies provide tools that inform teachers about specific ways of using formative assessment information to provide differentiated instruction.

The Panel also recommends that research be conducted regarding the content and criterion-related validity and reliability of other types of formative assessments (such as unit mastery tests included with many published mathematics programs, performance assessments, and dynamic assessments involving "think alouds"). This research should include studies of consequential validity (i.e., the impact they have on helping teachers improve their effectiveness).

Use of formative assessments in mathematics can lead to increased precision in how instructional time is used in class and can assist teachers in identifying specific instructional needs. Formative measures provide guidance as to the specific topics needed for assistance. Formative assessment should be an integral component of instructional practice in mathematics.

TEACHING LOW-ACHIEVING STUDENTS AND STUDENTS WITH LEARNING DISABILITIES

The Panel conducted a review of 26 high-quality studies, mostly using randomized control designs. These studies provide a great deal of guidance concerning some defining features of effective instructional approaches for students with learning disabilities (LD) as well as low-achieving (LA) students. The review indicated that explicit methods of instruction are effective with LD and LA students.

Some key findings:

- Explicit systematic instruction was found to improve the performance of students with learning disabilities in computation, solving word problems, and solving problems that require the application of mathematics to novel situations. *Explicit systematic instruction* typically entails teachers explaining and demonstrating specific strategies and allowing students many opportunities to ask and answer questions and to think aloud about the decisions they make while solving problems. It also entails careful sequencing of problems by the teacher or through instructional materials to highlight critical features. Significant positive effects were also found for Direct Instruction (a specific type of explicit instruction that provides teachers with scripts and that calls for frequent interactions between students and teachers, clear feedback to students on the accuracy of their work, and sequencing of problems so that critical differences are highlighted). Other forms of explicit systematic instruction have been developed with applications for students with learning disabilities. These developments reflect the infusion of research findings from cognitive psychology, with particular emphasis on automaticity and enhanced problem representation.

- Most of the small number of studies that investigated the use of visual representations yielded nonsignificant effects. However, studies that included visual representations along with the other components of explicit instruction tended to produce significant positive effects.

Recommendation: **The Panel recommends that students with learning disabilities and other students with learning problems receive, on a regular basis, some explicit systematic instruction that includes opportunities for students to ask and answer questions and think aloud about the decisions they make while solving problems. This kind of instruction should not comprise all the mathematics instruction these students receive. However, it does seem essential for building proficiency in both computation and the translation of word problems into appropriate mathematical equations and solutions. Some of this time should be dedicated to ensuring that students possess the foundational skills and conceptual knowledge necessary for understanding the mathematics they are learning at their grade level.**

Recommendation: **The Panel identified surprisingly few methodologically rigorous studies (given a literature base that spanned the past 30 years) that examined instructional practices designed to improve the performance of low-achieving students and students with learning disabilities. Although the actual quantity of such studies was small, their quality was high. There is a critical need for stimulating and supporting through federal funding of additional high-quality research to address this major national challenge.**

USING 'REAL-WORLD' PROBLEMS TO TEACH MATHEMATICS

The Panel's review of the literature addressed the question of whether using "real-world" contexts to introduce and teach mathematical topics and procedures is preferable to using more typical instructional approaches. The meaning of the term "real-world" problem varies by mathematician, researcher, developer, and teacher. Doing research in this area is complex; fidelity of the teachers' implementation of the instructional materials or instructional strategy is difficult to assess; contextual features, such as socioeconomic status or the school's orientation toward reform, matter and, most likely, although not addressed in the studies examined by the Panel, teachers' knowledge and capacity to use such problems effectively varies greatly.

The body of high-quality studies on this topic is small. We located 10 studies that met our criteria for quality. Five of these addressed the question of whether the use of "real-world" problems as the instructional approach led to improved performance on outcome measures of ability to solve "real-world" problems, as well as on more traditional assessments. Four of these were similar enough to combine in a meta-analysis. They involved upper elementary and middle school students, as well as ninth-grade remedial students; the mathematical topics included fraction computation and beginning equation solving. The analysis revealed that if mathematical ideas are taught using "real-world" contexts, then students' performance on assessments involving similar problems is improved. However, performance on assessments of other aspects of mathematics learning, such as computation, simple word problems, and equation solving, is not improved.

For certain populations (upper elementary and middle grade students, and remedial ninth-graders) and for specific domains of mathematics (fraction computation, basic equation solving, and function representation), instruction that features the use of "real-world" contexts has a positive impact on certain types of problem solving. However, these results are not sufficient as a basis for widespread policy recommendations. Additional research is needed to explore the use of "real-world" problems in other mathematical domains, at other grade levels, and with varied definitions of "real-world" problems.

TECHNOLOGY AND APPLICATIONS OF TECHNOLOGY: CALCULATORS AND COMPUTER-BASED INSTRUCTION

Although young in historic terms, computer technology has a strong presence in people's lives and in the research literature. The Panel reviewed research on the role of technology, including computer software and calculators, in mathematics instruction and learning.

A review of 11 studies that met the Panel's rigorous criteria (only one study less than 20 years old) found limited or no impact of calculators on calculation skills, problem solving, or conceptual development over periods of up to 1 year. This finding is limited to the effect of calculators as used in the 11 studies. Unfortunately, these studies cannot be used to judge the advantages or disadvantages of multiyear calculator use beginning in the early years because such long-term use has not been adequately investigated.

The Panel's survey of the nation's algebra teachers indicated that the use of calculators in prior grades was one of their concerns (National Mathematics Advisory Panel, 2008). The Panel cautions that to the degree that calculators impede the development of automaticity, fluency in computation will be adversely affected.

Recommendation:	**The Panel recommends that high-quality research on particular uses of calculators be pursued, including both their short- and long-term effects on computation, problem solving, and conceptual understanding.**

Research on instructional software has generally shown positive effects on students' achievement in mathematics as compared with instruction that does not incorporate such technologies. These studies show that technology-based drill and practice and tutorials can improve student performance in specific areas of mathematics. Other studies show that teaching computer programming to students can support the development of particular mathematical concepts, applications, and problem solving.

However, the nature and strength of the results vary widely across these studies. In particular, one recent large, multisite national study found no significant effects of instructional tutorial (or tutorial and practice) software when implemented under typical conditions of use. Taken together, the available research is insufficient for identifying the factors that influence the effectiveness of instructional software under conventional circumstances.

> **Recommendation:** **The Panel recommends that high-quality computer-assisted instruction (CAI) drill and practice, implemented with fidelity, be considered as a useful tool in developing students' automaticity (i.e., fast, accurate, and effortless performance on computation), freeing working memory so that attention can be directed to the more complicated aspects of complex tasks.**

Research has demonstrated that tutorials (i.e., CAI programs, often combined with drill and practice) that are well designed and implemented can have a positive impact on mathematics performance, particularly at the middle and high school levels. CAI tutorials have been used effectively to introduce and teach new subject-matter content. Research suggests that tutorials that are designed to help specific populations meet specific educational goals have a positive impact. However, these studies also suggest several important caveats. Care must be taken to ensure that there is evidence that the software to be used has been shown to increase learning in the specific domain and with students who are similar to those who will use the software. Educators should critically inspect individual software packages and the studies that evaluate them. Furthermore, the requisite support conditions to use the software effectively (sufficient hardware and software; technical support; adequate professional development, planning, and curriculum integration) should be in place, especially in large-scale implementations, to achieve optimal results.

> **Recommendation:** **The Panel recommends that high-quality computer-assisted instruction (CAI) tutorials, implemented with fidelity, be considered as a potentially useful tool in introducing and teaching specific subject-matter content to specific populations. The Panel also recommends that additional high-quality research be pursued to identify which goals and which populations are served well by tutorials, as well as the**

particular features of effective tutorials and of their implementation in the classroom.

Research indicates that learning to write computer programs improves students' performance compared to conventional instruction, with the greatest effects on understanding of concepts and applications, especially geometric concepts, and weaker effects on computation. However, computer programming by students can be employed in a wide variety of situations using distinct pedagogies, not all of which may be effective. Therefore, the findings are limited to the careful, targeted application of computer programming for learning used in the studies reviewed.

Recommendation:	**The Panel recommends that computer programming be considered as an effective tool, especially for elementary school students, for developing specific mathematics concepts and applications, and mathematical problem-solving abilities. Effects are larger if the computer programming language is designed for learning (e.g., Logo) and if students' programming is carefully guided by teachers so as to explicitly teach students to achieve specific mathematical goals.**

There are insufficient rigorous studies of other categories of software to make recommendations about their use. Problem-solving software may have potential, but more research is needed on this category of software, as well as on the effects of simulations, games, and Internet applications.

Finally, research is needed on specific features of software that theoretically should contribute to learning. Information regarding critical features of software is important, because decisions about whether to use existing software and how to develop new software could be guided by the software's inclusion or omission of these critical features. More research is also needed on issues relevant to software use, such as fidelity of implementation, curriculum integration, and use software as a replacement or supplement to other instruction.

TEACHING MATHEMATICALLY GIFTED STUDENTS

The Panel's review of the literature about what kind of mathematics instruction would be most effective for gifted students focused on the impact of programs involving acceleration, enrichment, and the use of homogeneous grouping. Although many syntheses and summaries of research in these areas have been conducted, our searches yielded surprisingly few studies that met the Panel's methodologically rigorous criteria for inclusion; thus for this section we relaxed these criteria to fulfill the charge of evaluating the "best available scientific evidence." The Panel could formulate its recommendations only on the basis of one randomized control trial study and seven quasi-experimental studies. These studies have limitations. For instance, motivation is a confounding variable, just as it is a selection criterion for being considered a candidate for acceleration.

The Panel's key findings are the following:

- The studies reviewed provided some support for the value of differentiating the mathematics curriculum for students with sufficient motivation, especially when acceleration is a component (i.e., pace and level of instruction are adjusted).
- A small number of studies indicated that individualized instruction, in which pace of learning is increased and often managed via computer instruction, produces gains in learning.
- Gifted students who are accelerated by other means not only gained time and reached educational milestones earlier (e.g., college entrance) but also appear to achieve at levels at least comparable to those of their equally able same-age peers on a variety of indicators even though they were younger when demonstrating their performance on the various achievement benchmarks.
- Gifted students appeared to become more strongly engaged in science, technology, engineering, or mathematical areas of study. There is no evidence in the research literature that gaps and holes in knowledge have occurred as a result of student acceleration.

In the case of gifted (or academically advanced) students who are advanced in their skill and concept attainment and can learn new material at a much more rapid rate than their same-age peers, it is the professional judgment of those in gifted education that they need a curriculum that is differentiated (by level, complexity, breadth, and depth), developmentally appropriate, and conducted at a more rapid rate.

Support also was found for supplemental enrichment programs. Of the two programs analyzed, one explicitly utilized acceleration as a program component and the other did not. Self-paced instruction supplemented with enrichment yielded the greater benefits. This supports the widely held view in the field of gifted education that combined acceleration and enrichment should be the intervention of choice.

Recommendation: **Mathematically gifted students with sufficient motivation appear to be able to learn mathematics much faster than students proceeding through the curriculum at a normal pace, with no harm to their learning, and should be allowed to do so.**

There is a need for more high-quality experimental and quasi-experimental research to study the effectiveness of interventions designed to meet the learning needs of gifted students. Especially vital are evaluations of academically rigorous enrichment programs.

It is important for school policies to support appropriately challenging work in mathematics for gifted and talented students. Acceleration, combined with enrichment, is a promising practice that is moderately well supported by the research literature, especially when the full range of available literature is considered.

End Note

[1] The detailed work underlying this section was carried out by the Task Group on Instructional Practices, whose report carries relevant references and more elaborate discussion (National Mathematics Advisory Panel, 2008).

In: Success in Mathematics Education   ISBN: 978-1-60692-299-6
Editor: Caroline B. Baumann   © 2009 Nova Science Publishers, Inc.

Chapter 8

INSTRUCTIONAL MATERIALS

United States Department of Education

ACCURACY OF TEXTBOOKS

One would like to assume that textbooks for middle school and high school mathematics are free of errors.[1] But when mathematicians have reviewed recently published middle and high school textbooks, they have identified many errors and a large number of ambiguous and confusing statements and problems. One such review of widely used Algebra I textbooks was conducted on behalf of the Panel. Many of the detected errors and ambiguities arose in word problems that were intended to elicit use of the mathematical concepts and procedures in "real-world" contexts.

Recommendation: **Publishers must ensure the mathematical accuracy of their materials. Those involved with developing mathematics textbooks and related instructional materials need to engage mathematicians, as well as mathematics educators, at all stages of writing, editing, and reviewing these materials.**

LENGTH, COHERENCE, AND SEQUENCING OF TOPICS

U.S. mathematics textbooks are extremely long. Not counting study guides and answers at the end of the books, middle and high school textbooks typically range from 600 to more than 900 pages. With the study guides and answers, they sometimes exceed 1,000 pages. Even elementary school textbooks sometimes exceed 700 pages. Mathematics textbooks were much shorter in previous decades and continue to be much shorter in many nations with higher mathematics achievement than in the United States. Thus, the great length is not needed for effective instruction. The excessive length also makes books unnecessarily expensive and difficult to transport between school and home, consequences that may undermine their effectiveness as tools for learning.

Recommendation: **All parties involved in the publication and adoption of textbooks should strive for more compact and more coherent mathematics texts for use by students in Grades K–8 and beyond.**

Textbook publishers emphasize that a major source of the textbooks' length is the need to cover all of the curricular expectations encompassed in any state's mathematics standards, as a topic covered in sixth grade in one state may be covered in seventh grade in another state and in eighth grade in a third state. This situation leads to the topic being included in all three grades' math textbooks. The large influence of this factor is illustrated by the fact that the state-specific editions of Algebra I textbooks published for California, Texas, and Florida are roughly 25% (more than 200 pages) shorter than the national edition published for the other 47 states. Coverage of all 50 states' benchmarks for a given grade increases length and decreases coherence—this despite the fact that mathematics is especially amenable to a coherent treatment. Integrating new concepts with previous ones is impossible when textbook writers cannot anticipate the topics students already have encountered.

Recommendation: **States and districts should strive for greater agreement regarding the topics to be emphasized and covered at particular grades. Textbook publishers should publish editions that include a clear emphasis on the material that these states and districts agree to teach in specific grades.**

Another source of lack of coherence and potential confusion in some textbooks is the table of contents. Tables of contents should provide students, teachers, and textbook adoption teams with a sense of the organization of the mathematical topics in the book. In some textbooks, however, tables of contents emphasize not the mathematics but rather specific applications (e.g., Ferris wheels, penny jars). Tables of contents that emphasize the mathematical content seem more likely to help teachers and students appreciate the coherence inherent in mathematics.

Other potentially useful ways of decreasing length and increasing coherence are: 1) reducing the number of photographs that are not essential to the mathematical content; 2) placing content aimed at providing extended review, enrichment activities, or motivation in supplements rather than in the main textbook; and 3) reducing applications in which the primary challenge is posed by the social studies or science content.

End Note

[1] The detailed work underlying this section was carried out by the Subcommittee on Instructional Materials, whose report carries relevant references and more elaborate discussion (National Mathematics Advisory Panel, 2008).

In: Success in Mathematics Education   ISBN: 978-1-60692-299-6
Editor: Caroline B. Baumann   © 2009 Nova Science Publishers, Inc.

Chapter 9

ASSESSMENT OF MATHEMATICS LEARNING

United States Department of Education

Achievement tests are widely used to estimate what students know and can do in specific subject areas.[1] Tests make visible to teachers, parents, and policymakers some of the outcomes of student learning. They also can drive instruction. Due to their important role in education today, the Panel examined released items from the mathematics portions of the NAEP and six state tests and reviewed the relevant scientific literature on the appropriate content of such tests, the setting of performance categories (e.g., by determining cut scores), and factors affecting the quality of measurement, accuracy, and appropriate test design.

On the basis of the work of the Task Group on Assessment, the Panel developed two broad recommendations that lead to several specific recommendations:

Recommendation:	**NAEP and state tests for students through Grade 8 should focus on and adequately represent the Panel's Critical Foundations of Algebra. Student achievement on this critical mathematics content should be reported and tracked over time.**
Recommendation:	**State tests and NAEP must be of the highest mathematical and technical quality. To this end, states and NAEP should develop procedures for item development, quality control, and oversight**

to ensure that test items reflect the best item-design features, are of the highest mathematical and psychometric quality, and measure what is intended, with non-construct-relevant sources of variance in performance minimized (i.e., with nonmathematical sources of influence on student performance minimized).

These recommendations are not independent of each other. What one tests and how one chooses to test are intertwined. The background for these recommendations is discussed in this section, and additional specific recommendations are presented.

CONTENT

The mathematical content strands in many state tests are highly similar to those in the NAEP tests, although there are striking differences in the weights attached to these strands. Thus, the Panel focused its investigation on the NAEP content strands, knowing that any suggestions for the NAEP would have implications for state mathematics tests as well.

Table 3 shows the Panel's recommended content strands for NAEP's mathematics assessments. This new structure is intended to ensure that the content strands address what students should be learning. In the Panel's view, this begins with the Critical Foundations of Algebra.

Table 3. Suggested Reorganization of NAEP Content Strands

Grade 4	Grade 8
Number: Whole Numbers	Number: Integers
Number: Fractions and Decimals	Number: Fractions, Decimals, and Percent
Geometry and Measurement	Geometry and Measurement
Algebra	Algebra
Data Display	Data Analysis and Probability

Because the most critical skills leading to Algebra concern whole numbers, whole-number operations, and facility with fractions, we make the following recommendation:

Recommendation: **The Panel suggests that the NAEP strand on "Number Properties and Operations" be expanded and divided into two parts. The first part should include a focus on whole numbers, including whole number operations (i.e., addition, subtraction, multiplication, division), at Grade 4, and on all integers (negative and positive) at Grade 8. The second content area involving number should focus on fractions. At Grade 4, it should involve beginning work with fractions and decimals, including recognition, representation, and comparing and ordering. The coverage should be expanded to include operations with fractions, decimals and percent at Grade 8. Similarly, the content of work with whole numbers and fractions on state tests should expand and also should cover these concepts and operations as they develop from year to year, particularly at Grades 5, 6, and 7, which are grade levels when the NAEP test is not offered.**

One of the Panel's greatest concerns is that fractions are underrepresented on NAEP. The NAEP Validity Study (NVS; Daro et al., 2007), as well as others, have noted the relative paucity of items assessing fractions, particularly within the Grade 8 NAEP. (And, teachers have noted the importance of ensuring proficiency with fractions before beginning the study of algebra; see the Panel-commissioned National Survey of Algebra Teachers, National Mathematics Advisory Panel, 2008.) Moreover, Daro et al. indicate that half of the Data Analysis and Probability section in the Grade 4 NAEP test is probability-related. Given the importance of fractions for the conceptual understanding of probability, the Panel questions the appropriateness of items related to probability within NAEP at Grade 4. Thus, the Panel recommends that this strand at Grade 4 emphasize well-organized representations of data pictorially and numerically and be re-titled as "Data Display."

The Panel also recommends a more appropriate balance in how algebra is defined and assessed in both the Grade 4 and Grade 8 NAEP. At Grade 4, most of the NAEP algebra items relate to patterns or sequences (Daro et al., 2007). Although states' inclusion of patterns in textbooks or as curriculum expectations may reflect their views of what constitutes algebra, patterns are not emphasized in high-achieving countries (Schmidt, 2007). In the Major Topics of School Algebra set forth in this report, patterns are not a topic of major importance. The prominence given to patterns in PreK–8 is not supported by comparative analyses of curricula or mathematical considerations (Wu, 2007). Thus, the Panel strongly recommends that "algebra" problems involving patterns should be greatly reduced in the NAEP.

It should be noted that the TIMSS content domains were recently changed (Mullis et al., 2007), independent of the Panel's work. If the above recommendation was to be adopted by the National Assessment Governing Board, NAEP would be brought into greater alignment with TIMSS.

PERFORMANCE CATEGORIES

Once content is selected, decisions must be made as to what constitutes acceptable performance. The Panel did not investigate what the cut scores or standards ought to be, but rather looked at how they should be determined. Although the states and NAEP vary in both process and method for such standard setting, all six studied states and NAEP employ acceptable educational practices to quantify judgments of the standard-setting panelists and to map their judgments on to test scores.

The Panel examined the background of the panelists in NAEP and the six states and found that classroom teachers predominate, many of whom are not mathematics specialists. The panels used to set performance categories should draw on the expertise of mathematicians, mathematics educators, and curriculum specialists in education and academia, as well as of teachers and the general public. The Panel also found that the standard-setting panelists often do not take the complete test as examinees before attempting to set the performance categories, and that their judgments are not consistently informed by international performance data. Thus, the Panel also suggests that these deficiencies be addressed. On the basis of international performance data, there are indications that the NAEP cut scores for the two highest performance categories are set too high. This does not mean, however, that the mathematical content of the test is too hard; it is simply a statement about the location of cut scores for qualitative categories such as "proficient" and "beyond proficient."

Recommendation:	**Mathematicians should be included in greater numbers, along with mathematics educators, mathematics education researchers, curriculum specialists, classroom teachers, and the general public, in the standard-setting process and in the review and design of mathematical test items for state, NAEP, and commercial tests.**

ITEM AND TEST DESIGN

It is important not only that appropriate content is measured and cut scores for student proficiency are set appropriately, but also that test scores are valid and reliable, and reflect the competencies that are intended to be measured. That is, the measurement itself must be carried out in a high-quality and appropriate manner.

The Panel first examined whether constructed-response formats measure different aspects of mathematics competency in comparison with the multiple-choice format. Many educators believe that constructed-response items (e.g., short answers) are superior to multiple-choice items in measuring mathematical competencies and that they represent a more authentic measure of mathematical skill. The Panel examined the literature on the psychometric properties of constructed-response items as compared to multiple-choice items. The evidence in the scientific literature does not support the assumption that a constructed-response format, particularly the short-answer type, measures different aspects of mathematics competency in comparison with the multiple-choice format.

The Panel then examined test items for flaws. The NVS reported many examples of flawed and marginal items on NAEP and state assessments that could affect performance of all or some students (Daro et al., 2007). The Panel probed that issue in depth and also concluded that there are too many flawed items on the NAEP and state tests, often related to the wording of an item. The Panel classified the many flaws discovered in the individual test items into seven general types that could introduce non-construct-relevant variance (i.e., unwarranted nonmathematical sources of influence) and affect the meaning and accuracy of scores. The Panel recommends that test developers be especially sensitive to the presence of these types of flaws in the test development process. To further ameliorate concerns, significant attention should be devoted to the actual design of individual mathematics items and to the evaluation of items for inclusion in an assessment. Careful attention must be paid to exactly what mathematical knowledge is being assessed by a particular item and the extent to which the item is, in fact, focused on that mathematics. To that end, more mathematicians and mathematics educators should be involved in the test development process, as well as curriculum specialists, linguistics experts, and cognitive psychologists.

The frequency of flawed items on NAEP and state tests points to another possible gap in test development procedures that needs to be addressed. The developers of NAEP and state tests use sophisticated psychometric models and methods for this highly complex and technical process. Yet, it is the professional opinion of the Panel that problems in communication may be an additional contributing cause of the number of flawed items found in the NVS and by this Panel. Psychometricians are trained to use highly sophisticated statistical models and data analysis methods for measurement but are not as familiar with issues of designing items to measure specified constructs. In contrast, typical item writers and item evaluators have a college degree, but not always in the appropriate subject, and, typically, have little or no training in task and item design. Moreover, they often receive limited feedback from psychometricians on how the items they develop end up functioning. A more interactive feedback mechanism with more diagnostic information about item responses would help item writers pinpoint the sources of item flaws.

Use of calculators on assessments is another oft-discussed design issue. While findings from the literature indicated that using calculators on assessments has no significant short-term impact on performance overall or in problem solving, it does affect performance on computation-related items and could also change the nature of the competencies assessed.

Recommendation:	**Much more attention should be paid to the mathematical knowledge being assessed by a particular item and to the extent to which the item addresses that knowledge.**
Recommendation:	**Calculators should not be used on test items designed to assess computational facility.**

Research Needs

Recommendation: **More research is needed on test item design features and how they influence the measurement of the knowledge, skills, and abilities that students use when solving mathematics problems on achievement tests. These design features might have differential impacts across various groups (e.g., gender, race, English language learners).**

End Note

[1] The detailed work underlying this section was carried out by the Task Group on Assessment whose report carries relevant references and more elaborate discussion (National Mathematics Advisory Panel, 2008).

In: Success in Mathematics Education
Editor: Caroline B. Baumann

ISBN: 978-1-60692-299-6
© 2009 Nova Science Publishers, Inc.

Chapter 10

RESEARCH POLICIES AND MECHANISMS

United States Department of Education

Systematic reviews of research on mathematics education by the task groups and subcommittees of the Panel yielded thousands of studies on important topics, but only a small proportion met standards for rigor for the causal questions the Panel was attempting to answer. The dearth of relevant rigorous research in the field is a concern. First, the number of experimental studies in education that can provide answers to questions of cause and effect is currently small. Although the number of such studies has grown in recent years due to changes in policies and priorities at federal agencies, these studies are only beginning to yield findings that can inform educational policy and practice. Second, in educational research over the past two decades, the pendulum has swung sharply away from quantitative analyses that permit inferences from samples to populations. Third, there is a need for a stronger emphasis on such aspects of scientific rigor as operational definitions of constructs, basic research to clarify phenomena and constructs, and disconfirmation of hypotheses. Therefore, debates about issues of national importance, which mainly concern cause and effect, have devolved into matters of personal opinion rather than scientific evidence.

*Causal knowledge is essential to produce and to evaluate scientific research in crucial areas of national nee*d, including mathematics education. Specifically, research is needed that identifies: 1) effective instructional practices and materials, 2) mechanisms of learning, 3) ways to enhance teachers' effectiveness, including teacher education that focus on learning processes and outcomes, and 4) item and test features that improve the assessment of mathematical knowledge.

To achieve these goals, the rigor and scale of the federal government's infrastructure for educational research must be dramatically increased. In particular, the nation's research portfolio should be better diversified, increasing experimental research at multiple points along a continuum from smaller-scale (less costly but highly informative) experiments to large field trials that address problems of major national importance. And, to be ready for even small-scale experiments, basic research and intervention development studies are needed to bring interventions and models to a point such that studying their efficacy is viable.

Both smaller-scale experiments on the basic science of learning and larger-scale randomized experiments examining effective classroom practices are needed to ensure the coherent growth of research addressing important questions in mathematics education. Basic research on causal mechanisms of learning, as well as randomized trials, are essential, and, depending on their methodologies, both can be rigorous and relevant to educational practice. Basic research, in particular, is necessary to develop explicit predictions and to test hypotheses, which are underemphasized in current research on mathematics education.

There are three elements that are essential to produce the needed quality and quantity of research: 1) a sufficient supply of competent researchers dedicated to areas of critical national need; 2) a sufficient supply of willing schools and practitioners who have the time, resources, and motivation to be partners in research and to use the findings of research in decision making; and 3) a sufficient and stable source of funding for quality research and training with appropriate peer review. Streamlining human subjects' protection procedures for qualified, low-risk research would be a major factor in encouraging researchers to conduct educationally relevant research. In addition, the supply of researchers can be increased by improving the training of researchers in education, by encouraging qualified researchers from closely related fields to retrain in education, and by fostering collaborative, interdisciplinary research teams (such as those developed by the Social Science Research Council and others during the post-Sputnik period (Brown, 1970; Morrissett & Vinsonhaler, 1965)).

Recommendation:	Leaders of graduate programs in education and related fields should ensure attention to research design, analysis, and interpretation for teachers and those entering academic and educational leadership positions in order to increase the national capacity to conduct and utilize rigorous research.

Recommendation: **New funding should be provided to establish support mechanisms for career shifts (K, or career, awards from the National Institutes of Health represent one example). Many accomplished researchers who study the basic components of mathematics learning are not directly engaged in relevant educational research. While this more basic kind of research is important both in its own right and as a crucial foundation for designing classroom-level learning projects, at least some of these investigators have the potential to make more directly relevant contributions to educational research. Consequently, providing incentives for them to change the emphasis of their research programs could enhance research capacity in the field.**

Recommendation: **Support should be provided to encourage the creation of cross-disciplinary research teams, including expertise in educational psychology, sociology, economics, cognitive development, mathematics, and mathematics education.**

Recommendation: **PreK–12 schools should be provided with incentives and resources to provide venues for, and encourage collaboration in, educational research.**

Recommendation: **Unnecessary barriers to research should be lowered. Although existing guidelines for the protection of human subjects must be fully respected, Institutional Review Board procedures should be streamlined for educational research that qualifies as being of low or minimal risk. The resolutions of the National Board for Education Sciences concerning making individual student data available to researchers with appropriate**

safeguards for confidentiality should be supported.

In summary, to produce a steady supply of high-quality research that is relevant to classroom instruction, national capacity must be increased: More researchers in the field of mathematics education must be prepared, venues for research must be made accessible, and a pipeline of research must be funded that extends from the basic science of learning, to the rigorous development of materials and interventions to help improve learning, to field studies in classrooms. The most important criterion for this research is scientific rigor, ensuring trustworthy knowledge in areas of national need.

BIBLIOGRAPHY

Achieve, Inc. (2006). *Closing the expectations gap: An annual 50-state progress report on the alignment of high school policies with the demands of college and work.* Washington, DC: Author.

Adelman, C. (1999). Answers in the toolbox: Academic intensity, attendance patterns and bachelor's degree attainment. Washington, DC: U.S. Department of Education.

Anastasi, A. (1968). Psychological testing (3rd ed.). London: Collier-Macmillan Ltd.

Ashby, C. (2006). *Science, technology, engineering and math trends and the role of federal programs: A report to the Committee in Education and the Workforce, U.S. House of Representatives* (GAO-06-702T). Washington, DC: Government Accountability Office.

Babco, E. (2006). *Four decades of STEM degrees, 1966–2004: The devil is in the details.* Retrieved November 26, 2007, from http://www.cpst.org/ STEM/STEM6_Report.pdf.

Baldi, S., Jin, Y., Skemer, M., Green, P.J., Herget, D. & Xie, H., (2007). *Highlights from PISA 2006: Performance of U.S. 15-year-old students in science and mathematics literacy in an international context.* Washington, DC: U.S. Department of Education.

Bjork, R. A. (1994). Memory and meta-memory considerations in the training of human beings. In J. Metcalfe, & A. Shimamura (Eds.), *Metacognition: knowing about knowing* (pp. 185–205). Cambridge, MA: MIT Press.

Brown, R. (1970). *Cognitive development in children: Five monographs of the Society for Research in Child Development.* Chicago: University of Chicago Press.

Business Higher Education Forum (2005). *A commitment to America's future: Responding to the crisis in mathematics and science education.* Washington, DC: Author.

Carnevale, A. P. & Desrochers, D. M. (2003). Standards for what? The economic roots of K–16 reform. Washington, DC: Educational Testing Service.

Cook, T. D. & Campbell, D.T. (1979). *Quasi-experimentation: Design and analysis for field settings.* Chicago: Rand McNally.

Cronbach, L., & Meehl, P. (1955). Construct validity in psychological tests. *Psychological Bulletin*, 52, 281–302.

Daro, P., Stancavage, F., Ortega, M., DeStefano, L. & Linn, R. (2007). *Validity study of the NAEP mathematics assessment: Grades 4 and 8.* (Chapters 2 and 3). Washington, DC: American Institutes for Research. Retrieved on September 1, 2007 from http://www.air.org/publications/documents/NAEP_Math_Validity_Study.pdf.

Duschl, R. A., Schweingruber, H. A. & Shouse, A. W., (Eds.). (2007). *Taking science to school: Teaching and learning science in Grades K–8.* Washington, DC: National Academies Press.

Evan, A., Gray, T. & Olchefske, J. (2006). *The gateway to student success in mathematics and science.* Washington, DC: American Institutes for Research.

Ginsburg, A., Cooke, G., Leinwand, S. Noell, J. & Pollock, E. (2005). *Reassessing U.S. international mathematics performance: New findings from the 2003.* TIMSS and PISA. Washington, DC: American Institutes for Research.

Hecht, S. A., Vagi, K. J. & Torgesen, J. K. (2007). Fraction skills and proportional reasoning. In D. B. Berch & M. M. M. Mazzocco (Eds.), *Why is math so hard for some children? The nature and origins of mathematical learning difficulties and disabilities* (pp. 121–132). Baltimore: Paul H. Brookes Publishing Co.

Horn, L. & Nuñez, A. (2000). *Mapping the road to college: First-generation students' math track, planning strategies, and context of support* (NCES 2000-153). Washington, DC: U.S. Department of Education.

Horowitz, J.E. (2005). *Inside high school reform: Making the Changes that Matter.* San Francisco: WestEd.

Klein, D., Braams, B.J., Parker, T., Quirk, W., Schmid, W., & Wilson, W.S. (2005). *The state of state math standards 2005.* Thomas B. Fordham Institute. Retrieved on August 31, 2007 from http://www.edexcellence.net/foundation/publication/publication.cfm?id=338& pubsubid=1118#1118.

Lewin, K. (1951). Field theory in social science. *Selected theoretical papers.* New York: Harper & Row.

Mazzocco, M. M. M. & Devlin, K. T. (in press). Parts and holes: Gaps in rational number sense among children with vs. without mathematical learning disabilities. *Developmental Science.*

McGregor, E. (1994). *Economic development and public education: Strategies and standards. Educational Policy, 8(3),* 252–271.

Morrissett, L. D. & Vinsonhaler, J. (1965). *Mathematical learning: Report of a conference sponsored by the Committee on Intellective Processes Research of the Social Science Research Council.* Chicago: University of Chicago Press.

Mullis, I.V.S., Martin, M.O., Ruddock, G.J., O'Sullivan, C.Y., Arora, A., & Erberber, E. (2007). *TIMSS 2007 assessment frameworks.* Boston, MA: TIMSS & PIRLS International Study Center, Lynch School of Education, Boston College.

Murnane, R.J. & Levy, F. (1996). *Teaching the new basic skills: Principles for educating children to thrive in a changing economy.* Glencoe, IL: Free Press.

National Council of Teachers of Mathematics. (2006). *Curriculum focal points for prekindergarten through Grade 8 mathematics: A quest for coherence.* Reston, VA: National Council of Teachers of Mathematics.

National Mathematics Advisory Panel. (2008). *Reports of the Task Groups and Subcommittees.* Washington, DC: Author.

National Research Council. (2001). *Adding it up: Helping children learn mathematics.* In J. Kilpatrick, J. Swafford, & B. Findell (Eds.), Mathematics learning study committee, center for education, division of behavioral and social sciences, and education. Washington, DC: National Academies Press.

National Science Board. (2008). *Science and engineering indicators 2008. Two volumes.* Arlington, VA: National Science Foundation (Vol. 1, NSB 08-01; Vol. 2, NSB 08-01A).

National Science Board. (2003). *The science and engineering workforce: Realizing America's potential.* Arlington, VA: National Science Foundation (NSB 03-69).

National Science Foundation. (2007). *Asia's rising science and technology strength: Comparative indicators for Asia, the European Union, and the United States.* NSF 07-319. Arlington, VA: Author.

Pascarella, E. T. & Terenzini. P.T. (1991). *How college affects students: Findings and insights from twenty years of research, Vol. I.* San Francisco: Jossey-Bass.

Phillips, G. W. (2007). *Chance favors the prepared mind: Mathematics and science indicators for comparing states and nations.* Washington, DC: American Institutes for Research.

Platt, J. R. (1964). Strong inference. *Science, 146,* 347–353.

Roediger, H. L. & Karpiche, J.D. (2006). Test-enhanced Learning: Taking memory tests improves long-term retention. *Psychological Science, 17,* 249–255.

Schacht, W. H. (2005). *Industrial competitiveness and technological advancement: Debate over government policy* (Order Code IB91132). CRS Issue Brief for Congress. Washington, DC: Congressional Research Service.

Schmidt, W. H. & Houang, R. T. (2007). Lack of focus in mathematics: Symptom or cause? Lessons learned: In T. Loveless (Ed.), *What international assessments tell us about math achievement.* Washington, DC: Brookings Institution Press.

Shavelson, R. J. & Towne, L. (2002). *Scientific research in education.* Washington, DC: National Academy Press.

Shoenfeld, A. H. (1995). Report of working group 1. In C.B. Lacampagne, W. Blair, & J. Kaput (Eds.), (1995). *The algebra initiative colloquium, Vol. 2.* (p. 11). Washington DC: U.S. Department of Education.

Singapore Ministry of Education. (2006). Education at secondary schools. Retrieved on June 1, 2007 from http://www.moe.gov.sg/esp/ schadm/sec1/Edu_at_Sec_Schs.htm.

U.S. Department of Education. (1990–2007). *National Assessment of Educational Progress.* National Center for Educational Statistics. Retrieved on September 1, 2007 from http://nces.ed.gov/nationsreportcard/.

Wu, H. (2007). *Fractions, decimals, and rational numbers.* University of California, Department of Mathematics. Retrieved on February 1, 2008 from http://math.berkeley.edu/~wu/.

APPENDIX A: PRESIDENTIAL EXECUTIVE ORDER 13398

Presidential Documents

Executive Order 13398 of April 18, 2006

National Mathematics Advisory Panel

By the authority vested in me as President by the Constitution and the laws of the United States of America, it is hereby ordered as follows:

Section 1. *Policy.* To help keep America competitive, support American talent and creativity, encourage innovation throughout the American economy, and help State, local, territorial, and tribal governments give the Nation's children and youth the education they need to succeed, it shall be the policy of the United States to foster greater knowledge of and improved performance in mathematics among American students.

Sec. 2. *Establishment and Mission of Panel.* (a) There is hereby established within the Department of Education (Department) the National Mathematics Advisory Panel (Panel).

(b) The Panel shall advise the President and the Secretary of Education (Secretary) consistent with this order on means to implement effectively the policy set forth in section 1, including with respect to the conduct, evaluation, and effective use of the results of research relating to proven-effective and evidence-based mathematics instruction.

Sec. 3. *Membership and Chair of Panel.* (a) The Panel shall consist of no more than 30 members as follows:

(i) no more than 20 members from among individuals not employed by the Federal Government, appointed by the Secretary for such terms as the Secretary may specify at the time of appointment; and

(ii) no more than 10 members from among officers and employees of Federal agencies, designated by the Secretary after consultation with the heads of the agencies concerned.

(b) From among the members appointed under paragraph(3)(a)(i) of this order, the Secretary shall designate a Chair of the Panel.

(c) Subject to the direction of the Secretary, the Chair of the Panel shall convene and preside at meetings of the Panel, determine its agenda, direct its work and, as appropriate to deal with particular subject matters, establish and direct the work of subgroups of the Panel that shall consist exclusively of members of the Panel.

Sec. 4. *Report to the President on Strengthening Mathematics Education.* In carrying out subsection 2(b) of this order, the Panel shall submit to the President, through the Secretary, a preliminary report not later than January 31, 2007, and a final report not later than February 28, 2008. Both reports shall, at a minimum, contain recommendations, based on the best available scientific evidence, on the following:

(a) the critical skills and skill progressions for students to acquire competence in algebra and readiness for higher levels of mathematics;

(b) the role and appropriate design of standards and assessment in promoting mathematical competence;

(c) the processes by which students of various abilities and backgrounds learn mathematics;

(d) instructional practices, programs, and materials that are effective for improving mathematics learning;

(e) the training, selection, placement, and professional development of teachers of mathematics in order to enhance students' learning of mathematics;

(f) the role and appropriate design of systems for delivering instruction in mathematics that combine the different elements of learning processes, curricula, instruction, teacher training and support, and standards, assessments, and accountability;

(g) needs for research in support of mathematics education;

(h) ideas for strengthening capabilities to teach children and youth basic mathematics, geometry, algebra, and calculus and other mathematical disciplines;

(i) such other matters relating to mathematics education as the Panel deems appropriate; and

(j) such other matters relating to mathematics education as the Secretary may require.

Sec. 5. *Additional Reports.* The Secretary may require the Panel, in carrying out subsection 2(b) of this order, to submit such additional reports relating to the policy set forth in section 1 as the Secretary deems appropriate.

Sec. 6. *General Provisions.* (a) This order shall be implemented in a manner consistent with applicable law, including section 103 of the Department of Education Organization Act (20 U.S.C. 3403), and subject to the availability of appropriations.

(b) The Department shall provide such administrative support and funding for the Panel as the Secretary determines appropriate. To the extent permitted by law, and where practicable, agencies shall, upon request by the Secretary, provide assistance to the Panel.

(c) The Panel shall obtain information and advice as appropriate in the course of its work from:

(i) officers or employees of Federal agencies, unless otherwise directed by the head of the agency concerned;

(ii) State, local, territorial, and tribal officials;

(iii) experts on matters relating to the policy set forth in section 1;

(iv) parents and teachers; and

(v) such other individuals as the Panel deems appropriate or as the Secretary may direct.

(d) Members of the Panel who are not officers or employees of the United States shall serve without compensation and may receive travel expenses, including per diem in lieu of subsistence, as authorized by law for persons serving intermittently in Government service (5 U.S.C. 5701–5707), consistent with the availability of funds.

(e) Insofar as the Federal Advisory Committee Act, as amended (5 U.S.C. App.) (the "Act"), may apply to the administration of any portion of this order, any functions of the President under that Act, except that of reporting to the Congress, shall be performed by the Secretary in accordance with the guidelines issued by the Administrator of General Services.

(f) This order is not intended to, and does not, create any right or benefit, substantive or procedural, enforceable by any party at law or in equity against the United States, its departments, agencies, entities, officers, employees, or agents, or any other person.

Sec. 7. *Termination.* Unless hereafter extended by the President, this Advisory Panel shall terminate 2 years after the date of this order.

THE WHITE HOUSE,
April 18, 2006.

[FR Doc. 06–3865
Filed 4–20–06; 8:45 am]
Billing code 3195–01–P

APPENDIX B: ROSTERS OF PANEL MEMBERS, STAFF, AND CONSULTANTS

Panelists

- Larry R. Faulkner (Chair), President, Houston Endowment Inc.; President Emeritus, University of Texas at Austin
- Camilla Persson Benbow (Vice Chair), Patricia and Rodes Hart Dean of Education and Human Development, Peabody College, Vanderbilt University
- Deborah Loewenberg Ball, Dean, School of Education and William H. Payne Collegiate Professor, University of Michigan
- A. Wade Boykin, Professor and Director of the Graduate Program, Department of Psychology, Howard University
- Douglas H. Clements, Professor, Graduate School of Education, University at Buffalo, State University of New York (Began with the Panel March 19, 2007)
- Susan Embretson, Professor, School of Psychology, Georgia Institute of Technology (Began with the Panel March 19, 2007)
- Francis "Skip" Fennell, Professor of Education, McDaniel College
- Bert Fristedt, Morse-Alumni Distinguished Teaching Professor of Mathematics, University of Minnesota, Twin Cities (Began with the Panel March 19, 2007)
- David C. Geary, Curators' Professor, Department of Psychological Sciences, University of Missouri
- Russell M. Gersten, Executive Director, Instructional Research Group; Professor Emeritus, College of Education, University of Oregon
- Nancy Ichinaga, Former Principal, Bennett-Kew Elementary School, Inglewood, California (Served with the Panel through May 29, 2007)
- Tom Loveless, The Herman and George R. Brown Chair, Senior Fellow, Governance Studies, The Brookings Institution
- Liping Ma, Senior Scholar, The Carnegie Foundation for the Advancement of Teaching.
- Valerie F. Reyna, Professor of Human Development, Professor of Psychology, and Co-Director, Center for Behavioral Economics and Decision Research, Cornell University
- Wilfried Schmid, Dwight Parker Robinson Professor of Mathematics, Harvard University

- Robert S. Siegler, Teresa Heinz Professor of Cognitive Psychology, Carnegie Mellon University
- James H. Simons, President, Renaissance Technologies Corporation; Former Chairman, Mathematics Department, State University of New York at Stony Brook
- Sandra Stotsky, Twenty-First Century Chair in Teacher Quality, University of Arkansas; Member, Massachusetts State Board of Education
- Vern Williams, Mathematics Teacher, Longfellow Middle School, Fairfax County Public Schools, Virginia
- Hung-Hsi Wu, Professor of Mathematics, University of California at Berkeley

Ex Officio Members

- Irma Arispe, Assistant Director for Life Sciences and Acting Assistant Director for Social and Behavioral Sciences, Office of Science and Technology Policy, Executive Office of the President (Began with the Panel May 30, 2007)
- Daniel B. Berch, Associate Chief, Child Development and Behavior Branch and Director, Mathematics and Science Cognition and Learning Program, National Institute of Child Health and Human Development, National Institutes of Health
- Joan Ferrini-Mundy, Division Director, Division of Research on Learning in Formal and Informal Settings, National Science Foundation (On an Intergovernmental Personnel Act Assignment from Michigan State University. Began with the Panel January 16, 2007)
- Diane Auer Jones, Deputy to the Associate Director for Science, White House Office of Science and Technology Policy (Served with the Panel through May 23, 2007)
- Thomas W. Luce, III, Assistant Secretary for Planning, Evaluation, and Policy Development, U.S. Department of Education (Served with the Panel through November 1, 2006).
- Kathie L. Olsen, Deputy Director, National Science Foundation, (Served with the Panel through January 11, 2007)
- Raymond Simon, Deputy Secretary, U.S. Department of Education

- Grover J. "Russ" Whitehurst, Director, Institute of Education Sciences, U.S. Department of Education

U.S. Department of Education Staff

- Tyrrell Flawn, Executive Director, National Mathematics Advisory Panel, U.S. Department of Education
- Ida Eblinger Kelley, Special Assistant, National Mathematics Advisory Panel, U.S. Department of Education
- Jennifer Graban, Deputy Director for Research and External Affairs, National Mathematics Advisory Panel, U.S. Department of Education
- Marian Banfield, Deputy Director of Programs and Special Projects, National Mathematics Advisory Panel, U.S. Department of Education

Additional support was provided by the following: Anya Smith, Director of Special Events and the Events Team, Office of Communications and Outreach, U.S. Department of Education; Holly Clark, Management and Program Analyst, Office of Innovation and Improvement, U.S. Department of Education; Mike Kestner, Math and Science Partnership Program, Office of Elementary and Secondary Education, U.S. Department of Education; Kenneth Thomson, Presidential Management Fellow, Office of Planning, Evaluation, and Policy Development, U.S. Department of Education; and Jim Yun, Math and Science Partnership Program, Office of Elementary and Secondary Education, U.S. Department of Education.

Consultants

- Alina Martinez, Abt Associates, Inc., Project Director
- Ellen Bobronnikov, Abt Associates, Inc.
- Fran E. O'Reilly, Abt Associates, Inc.
- Mark Lipsey, Vanderbilt University
- Pamela Flattau, Institute for Defense Analyses Science and Technology Policy Institute, Project Director
- Nyema Mitchell, Institute for Defense Analyses Science and Technology Policy Institute
- Kay Sullivan, Institute for Defense Analyses Science and Technology Policy Institute

- Jason Smith, Widmeyer Communications, Project Director
- Sara Appleyard, Widmeyer Communications
- Phyllis Blaunstein, Widmeyer Communications
- Alix Clyburn, Widmeyer Communications
- Jessica Love, Widmeyer Communications.79

APPENDIX C: ORGANIZATION AND OPERATION OF THE PANEL

The National Mathematics Advisory Panel (often called the "National Math Panel," NMP, or Panel) comprises 24 members designated by the Secretary of Education. Nineteen of the members are experts not employed by the federal government and five are ex officio designees from federal agencies. The members were sworn into service and the Panel began its work on May 22, 2006.

Some key dates in the Panel's work are as follows:

- April 18, 2006—Establishment of the National Mathematics Advisory Panel through Executive Order 13398
- May 15, 2006—Secretary Spellings announces Panel members
- May 22, 2006—Panel members sworn into service
- January 11, 2007—Preliminary report filed and accepted by the Panel
- March 13, 2008—Official release of the Final Report

Panel Meetings

Twelve meetings were held around the country as detailed in Appendix D. Please refer to the U.S. Department of Education Web site for more information about the meetings: http://www.ed.gov/about/bdscomm/list/mathpanel/meetings.html.

At most meetings, the Panel used a portion of its time working in task groups with the balance in public sessions, receiving testimony and holding preliminary public discussions about progress in the task groups. Much of the testimony was organized by the Panel to cover particular topics, such as textbooks, TIMSS, NAEP, and the use of technology, but a portion was allocated to open testimony on a first-come, first-served basis by individual members of the public or interested organizations. Seventy-one people provided public testimony through the meeting of October 2007. The meetings in November and December 2007 were entirely dedicated to reports from task groups and to the synthesis of this Final Report. All work at these later meetings was carried out in public sessions. The proceedings of all meetings have been recorded and documented through extensive minutes. Please refer to U.S. Department of Education Web site for more information on the public testimony received: http://www.ed.gov/about/bdscomm/list/mathpanel/index.html.

Organizations likely to have an interest in the Panel's work were contacted by mail to inform them of the work plan, and to solicit their advice and comments on matters of particular concern. In December 2006 and October 2007, the Department invited these stakeholders to briefings in Washington, D.C., at which the Chair discussed the Panel's process and progress and answered questions from attendees.

Task Groups and Subcommittees

The Panel chose to divide into task groups focused on detailed examination of topics set forth in the Executive Order. The full range of issues was covered in a phased process, with new efforts undertaken as earlier issues were completed. Subcommittees were charged with completion of a particular advisory function for the Panel. The task groups and subcommittees reported periodically to the entire Panel. Their work products were reviewed in progress by the Panel as a whole and were formally received by the Panel when completed; however, the reports of task groups and subcommittees are presented by only those members who participated in creating them. As described below, the Panel later incorporated some elements of these reports into this Final Report. These reporting documents are all available on the U.S. Department of Education Web site at http://www.ed.gov/about/bdscomm/list/ mathpanel/meetings.html.

The task groups and subcommittees were established as follows:

- Task Groups
  o Conceptual Knowledge and Skills
  o Learning Processes
  o Instructional Practices
  o Teachers and Teacher Education
  o Assessment

- Subcommittees
  o Standards of Evidence
  o Survey of Algebra I Teachers
  o Instructional Materials

Please refer to Appendix E for a roster of task group and subcommittee members.

Synthesis and Submission of This Report

The Panel as a whole synthesized this report, largely from the reports of the task groups and subcommittees. Three synthesis teams were appointed to develop parallel concepts for the Final Report, using the reports of the task groups and subcommittees as a basis. The team leaders then worked with the Chair and Vice Chair to set out a "common concept" for subsequent development by the Panel. The synthesis process began prior to the Phoenix, Arizona, public meeting and continued until the Final Report was adopted by the Panel as a whole.

The Panel submitted the Final Report to the Secretary of Education and the President of the United States on March 13, 2008. The Final Report was officially released to the public on that date, as well.

Standards of Evidence

The President's Executive Order called for the Panel to marshal the best available scientific evidence and offer advice on the effective use of the results of research related to proven, effective, and evidence-based mathematics instruction. The Panel's assertions and recommendations, therefore, are grounded in the highest-quality evidence available from scientific studies.

So that the Panel could be systematic in identifying the quality of evidence on which its assertions and recommendations were based, criteria for classifying evidence were developed through a two-level process. The Subcommittee on Standards of Evidence formulated general principles applicable to the Panel as a whole and to all of its task groups and subcommittees. In general, these principles call for strongest confidence to be placed in studies that

- Test hypotheses
- Meet the highest methodological standards (internal validity)
- Have been replicated with diverse samples of students under conditions that warrant generalization (external validity)

These principles are amplified in the excerpt from the subcommittee report at the end of this appendix. In addition, the Panel relied on expert professional judgment to address questions about the structure and content of mathematics as a subject and discipline.

The Report of the Subcommittee on Standards of Evidence is located with the reports of all task groups and subcommittees, and can be found on the U.S. Department of Education Web site at http://www.ed.gov/MathPanel.

Standards of evidence were developed and expressed in a more particular way at the task-group level, because the character and form of relevant evidence differ across the wide range of concerns addressed by the task groups. Accordingly, each task group report includes a detailed description of how the task group handled evidence in its particular substantive area. In effect, these sections show how the Panel-wide standards of evidence were manifested in the work of the individual groups.[1]

The task groups received support in their survey of the research literature and other relevant materials through contracts with Abt Associates and the Institute for Defense Analyses Science and Technology Policy Institute (IDA STPI). Abt carried out searches to capture high-quality, relevant research using criteria defined by each task group for its own needs. The results were examined directly by the task groups. The criteria set for searches were meant to exclude only clearly irrelevant sources. All final decisions about the rigor, adequacy, and inclusion of sources in the research literature were made exclusively by Panel members working in task groups. IDA STPI performed some original research and analysis using a variety of resources such as national reports and state education Web sites.

The Panel as a whole reviewed more than 16,000 research studies and related documents. Yet, only a small percentage of available research met the standards of evidence and could support conclusions.

Excerpt from the Report of the Subcommittee on Standards of Evidence

Background: Categories of Internal and External Validity

There are three broad categories into which one can categorize research and the corresponding claims based on that research. First, there is the highest quality scientific evidence, based on considerations such as the excellence of the design, the validity and reliability of measures, the size and diversity of student samples, and similar considerations of *internal* (scientific rigor and soundness) and *external* validity (generalizability to different circumstances and students). The importance of scientific theory and hypothesis testing, especially the active search for disconfirmation, cannot be overstated in judging the quality of research (see Platt,

1964). Furthermore, scientifically supported theory provides the surest path to generalization (Lewin, 1951). Hence, the Panel's strongest confidence will be reserved for studies that test hypotheses, that meet the highest methodological standards (internal validity), and that have been replicated with diverse samples of students under conditions that warrant generalization (external validity).

In addition to reviewing the best scientific evidence, the Panel is also charged with considering promising or suggestive findings that should be the subject of future research. Promising or suggestive studies do not meet the highest standards of scientific evidence, but they represent sound, scientific research that needs to be further investigated or extended. For example, laboratory studies showing significant effects of "desirable difficulties" (i.e., difficulties produced by challenging to-be-learned material) or of repeated testing on long-term retention could be extended to actual classrooms or existing curricula (e.g., Bjork, 1994; Roediger & Karpicke, 2004). The final category corresponds to statements based on values or weak evidence; these are essentially unfounded claims and will be designated as opinions as opposed to scientifically justified conclusions.

Quantity, Quality, and Balance of Evidence

Strong Evidence

All of the applicable high quality studies support a conclusion (statistically significant individual effects, significant positive mean effect size, or equivalent consistent positive findings) and they include at least three independent studies with different relevant samples and settings or one large high quality multisite study. Any applicable studies of less than high quality show either a preponderance of evidence consistent with the high quality studies (e.g., mean positive effect size) or such methodological weaknesses that they do not provide credible contrary evidence. Factors such as error variance and measurement sensitivity clearly influence the number of studies needed to support a conclusion (reflected in such statistics as p-rep, the probability of replicating an effect; Killeen, 2005); the number and balance of studies that are indicated above are, therefore, merely illustrative.

Moderately Strong Evidence

As above but there are fewer than three high quality studies (but at least one), or the effects have not been independently replicated by different researchers, or they do not involve different samples (i.e., diversity of characteristics) and settings.

Suggestive Evidence

One of the following:
- There are some high quality studies that support the conclusion (statistically significant effects, significant mean effects) but others that do not (nonsignificant), but those that do not are null, not negative (nonsignificant effect or mean effects but not significant negative effect). Any applicable moderate quality studies show a comparable pattern or better.
- There are no high quality studies, but all the applicable moderate quality studies support the conclusion (statistically significant individual effects, significant positive mean effect size, or equivalent consistent positive findings) and there are at least three such studies.

Inconsistent Evidence

The evaluation of mixed evidence depends crucially on the evaluation of the quality of the designs and methods of each study. The results of high-quality designs trump inconsistent or null results of low-quality designs. Mixed results of high and/or moderate quality studies that are not consistent enough to fall into any of the above categories, and cannot be adjudicated by methodological criteria, are inconclusive.

Weak Evidence

Evidence is considered weak when there are low quality studies but no applicable high or moderate quality studies.

To apply such criteria, the studies on which an assertion or recommendation is based must each be characterized as "high quality," "moderate quality," or "low quality." The standards for those designations will necessarily differ for the different kinds of research that are applicable to different issues and inferences (Shavelson & Towne, 2002). The primary interest of the Panel is experimental and quasi-experimental research designed to investigate the effects of programs, practices, and approaches on students' mathematics achievement. On some matters, however, the relevant studies are surveys (e.g., of students' mathematical knowledge). On other matters, the relevant sources represent compilations of practice and informed opinion (e.g., regarding the mathematical concepts essential to algebra). The methodological quality of individual studies will be categorized as part of the documentation for the database for the panel's work using definitions such as the following.

For studies of the effects of interventions:

High quality. Random assignment to conditions; low attrition (<20%); valid and reliable measures.

Moderate quality. Nonrandom assignment to conditions with matching, statistical controls, or a demonstration of baseline equivalence on important variables; low attrition or evidence that attrition effects are small; valid and reliable measures. Correlational modeling with instrumental variables and strong statistical controls. Random assignment studies with high attrition.

Low quality. Nonrandom assignment without matching or statistical controls. Pre-post studies. Correlational modeling without strong statistical controls. Quasi-experimental studies with high attrition.

For descriptive surveys of population characteristics:

High quality. Probability sampling of a defined population; low nonresponse rate
(< 20%) or evidence that nonresponse is not biasing; large sample (achieved sample size gives adequate error of estimate for the study purposes); valid and reliable measures.

Moderate quality. Purposive sampling from a defined population, face valid for representativeness; low nonresponse rate; moderate to large sample size; valid and reliable measures. Probability sample with high nonresponse rate but evidence that nonresponse is not biasing.

Low quality. Convenience sample; high nonresponse rate or evidence that it is biasing; small sample size; invalid or unreliable measures.

For studies of tests and assessments:

Psychometric standards such as measures of validity, reliability, and sensitivity will be used to evaluate tests and assessments (e.g., Anastasi, 1968; Cronbach & Meehl, 1955).

End Note

[1] The Report of the Subcommittee on Standards of Evidence also contains brief summaries of these sections from the task group reports.

APPENDIX D: DATES AND LOCATIONS OF MEETINGS

May 22, 2006—Washington, D.C.
Hosted by the National Academy of Sciences

June 28–29, 2006—Chapel Hill, North Carolina
Hosted by the University of North Carolina at Chapel Hill

September 13–14, 2006—Cambridge, Massachusetts
Hosted by Massachusetts Institute of Technology

November 5–7, 2006—Palo Alto, California
Hosted by Stanford University

January 10–11, 2007—New Orleans, Louisiana
Hosted by Xavier University of Louisiana

April 19–20, 2007—Chicago, Illinois
Hosted by Fermi National Accelerator Laboratory

June 5–6, 2007—Miami, Florida
Hosted by Miami Dade College

September 5–7, 2007—St. Louis, Missouri
Hosted by Washington University in St. Louis

October 23–24, 2007—Phoenix, Arizona
Hosted by Arizona State University

November 28, 2007—Baltimore, Maryland

December 14–15, 2007—Baltimore, Maryland

March 13, 2008—Falls Church, Virginia
Hosted by Longfellow Middle School

APPENDIX E: ROSTERS OF TASK GROUPS AND SUBCOMMITTEES

Task Groups

- Conceptual Knowledge and Skills
  - Francis "Skip" Fennell, Chair
  - Larry R. Faulkner
  - Liping Ma
  - Wilfried Schmid
  - Sandra Stotsky
  - Hung-Hsi Wu

- Learning Processes
  - David C. Geary, Chair
  - Wade Boykin
  - Susan E. Embretson (Beginning March 19, 2007)
  - Valerie F. Reyna
  - Robert S. Siegler
  - Daniel B. "Dan" Berch

- Instructional Practices
  - Russell M. Gersten, Co-Chair
  - Joan Ferrini-Mundy, Co-Chair (Beginning January 16, 2007)
  - Camilla Benbow
  - Douglas H. Clements (Beginning March 19, 2007)
  - Tom Loveless
  - Vern Williams
  - Irma Arispe (Beginning May 30, 2007)
  - Diane Auer Jones (Through May 23, 2007)

- Teachers and Teacher Education
  - Deborah Loewenberg Ball, Chair
  - James H. Simons
  - Hung-Hsi Wu
  - Raymond Simon
  - Grover J. "Russ" Whitehurst

- Assessment
  - o Camilla Persson Benbow, Chair
  - o Susan E. Embretson (Beginning March 19, 2007)
  - o Francis "Skip" Fennell
  - o Bert Fristedt (Beginning March 19, 2007)
  - o Tom Loveless
  - o Wilfried Schmid
  - o Sandra Stotsky
  - o Irma Arispe (Beginning May 30, 2007).

Subcommittees

- Standards of Evidence
  - o Valerie F. Reyna, Chair
  - o Camilla Persson Benbow
  - o Wade Boykin
  - o Grover J. "Russ" Whitehurst

- Survey of Algebra I Teachers
  - o Tom Loveless, Chair
  - o Deborah Loewenberg Ball
  - o Francis "Skip" Fennell
  - o Vern Williams

- Instructional Materials
  - o Robert S. Siegler, Chair
  - o Bert Fristedt
  - o Vern Williams
  - o Irma Arispe
  - o Daniel B. Berch

CHAPTER SOURCES

The following chapters have been previously published:

Chapters 1-10 - These are an edited, reformatted and augmented version of a United States Department of Education Contract No. E04CO0082/0001 publication, dated March 2008.

INDEX

D

I

J

K

L

Q

R